*Get Ahead!*
*Stay Ahead!*

# Get Ahead!
# Stay Ahead!

Learn the 70 Most Important
Career Skills, Traits, and Attitudes to
*Stay Employed!*
*Get Promoted!*
*Get a Better Job!*

**Dianna Booher**

**McGraw-Hill**

New York   San Francisco   Washington, D.C.   Auckland   Bogotá
Caracas   Lisbon   London   Madrid   Mexico City   Milan
Montreal   New Delhi   San Juan   Singapore
Sydney   Tokyo   Toronto

**Library of Congress Cataloging-in-Publication Data**

Booher, Dianna Daniels.
    Get ahead! Stay ahead! : learn the 70 most important career skills, traits, and attitudes to stay employed! Get a better job! / Dianna Booher.
              p.    cm.
    Includes bibliographical references
    ISBN 0-07-006648-5
    1. Career development.    2. Vocational guidance.    I. Title.
HF5381.B63516        1997
650.14—dc21                                              97-9261
                                                            CIP

# McGraw-Hill

A Division of The **McGraw·Hill** Companies

1  2  3  4  5  6  7  8  9  0  FGR / FGR  9  0  2  1  0  9  8  7

ISBN 0-07-006648-5

*The sponsoring editor for this book was Betsy N. Brown, the editing supervisor was Fred Dahl, and the production supervisor was Tina Cameron. This book was set in New Century Schoolbook by Inkwell Publishing Services.*

*Printed and bound by Quebecor Fairfield Graphics.*

McGraw-Hill books are available at special quantity discounts to use as premiums and sales promotions, or for use in corporate training programs. For more information, please write to the Director of Special Sales, McGraw-Hill, 11 West 19th Street, New York, NY 10011. Or contact your local bookstore.

 This book is printed on recycled, acid-free paper containing a minimum of 50% recycled, de-inked fiber.

# Contents

**v**

# *Acknowledgments*

Thanks to the following people who have contributed to this project so capably:

Heather MacKenzie (manuscript preparation)

Sandy Daniels (valuable insights)

Vernon Rae (editing and valuable insights)

Betsy Brown (my editor, suggesting the overall layout of information)

Greg Johnson (my agent, keeping all the balls of my various writing projects in the air)

# So Why Should You Care?

## Introduction

Too many people work too hard at their jobs—and not hard enough at their careers. That's a problem because jobs come and go, but a career keeps food on your table. A career gives you control of your own future.

You're probably reading this book in either of two states of mind—you're deliriously happy or you're decidedly disappointed. Let's hope it's the first condition.

You've accessed your spreadsheet and figured out that you're never going to get rich on someone else's payroll—unless you're already pretty near the top of the ladder. So you've left your "secure" job to strike out on your own for fame and fortune. You may be ready to incorporate yourself and start business on a grand scale with serious financial backing.

Or, you may be simply testing the waters in your mind. That is, you've taken one of those early-retirement buyout packages from your company and then contracted yourself to your old employer to complete a project or two. And while you're sitting on a little nest egg, you may intend to contract with a few other clients to offer them a specific skill or skills you've fine-tuned over the years.

If money isn't the motivator, maybe it is a sense of adventure, control, or balance in your life. You may have awakened one morning recently with the tempting idea of taking the day off to spend time with your family, get a massage, or play a round of golf without having to ask or tell anyone. The prompter varies from person to person.

You may still be on someone else's payroll because you love your job, and reading this book represents a yen to get yourself prepared for a promotion. You need to check your skills against those required for the raise and increased responsibilities.

In any of the above cases, you're deliriously happy with your present situation. You are a corporate survivor, but you have the good sense to plan ahead and take control of your future before someone else does it for you.

Then there's the other mind-set: decidedly disappointed. Your company or department has been rightsized, reengineered, or raided, and you're headed for a long job search. According to a 1996 survey of 1,885 executives by executive search firm Paul Ray Berndtson and Cornell University, 35 percent of executives feel dissatisfied with their jobs. Why? They're stressed from the heavier workload and pessimism about their employer's future.

It's not just the corporate execs who are restless. Those independent professionals, like lawyers, consultants, and psychologists, face new insecurities. According to the American Bar Association, the number of practicing attorneys keeps rising—their numbers have increased 25 percent in the last seven years. Competitiveness among their ranks runs rampant. Lawyers, consequently, have begun rethinking their skill sets. They have superb oral and written skills, are adept at setting priorities, can manage time, and can think analytically. If not law, where else can they use such skills?

For psychologists in private practice, the same rethinking has surfaced. The changes in healthcare brought on by managed care has them perplexed about how to compete. So, some are wondering, why limit myself by the "psychologist" shingle on my doorpost? Can I go to work inside the halls of corporate America?

Aerospace engineers find themselves in a similar predicament. For example, the Seattle-based Boeing Company, along with other majors, has departed from its past practice of looking for experienced engineers. In the company's latest round of hiring, Boeing's announcement headline read, "Even if you've never touched an airplane, you may have what it takes to join our team." The text continued with the explanation that rather than experience, they wanted new hires with mechanical aptitude, a good work ethic, and the ability to work on teams. "Previous experience" did not appear in the ad.

Lawyers, psychologists, engineers, teachers, techies, or tentmakers—all temporary jobs.

My point is this: Rethink yourself. Determine what skills you now have to market yourself. Acquire those you need. Then broaden your career goals—whether you're on someone else's payroll or your own.

This book will outline the skills, attitudes, and traits that will make you financially free for the future.

Human Resource professionals everywhere are collecting information on what hiring executives want to see in the people they hire. And leading-edge companies are collecting data on what skills, attitudes, and traits their frontline employees must have to earn customer satisfaction. In a sense, it is our customers or clients who "hire" us—every day with every project. So both bases—bosses and customers—are covered in this book.

To help determine your own skills, traits, or attitudes that will help you keep your job, find a job, or create your own job, look within—at your *own* security blanket.

## YOUR FUTURE SECURITY IS YOU

Let's face it. Companies can no longer afford to hire people for a lifetime. The world is changing too fast. IBM started out selling adding machines. Sears began with a mail-order house. General Electric started out providing only electricity. Technology changes. Customers *demand* change. Social and economic problems come and go.

To stay alive and profitable for their shareholders, companies have to take stock and reform themselves from time to time. Like an amoeba, they reach out and engulf people with certain skills and then they have to change forms to move around other obstacles placed in their growth path. If the company needs workers who can hold widgets between their toes while reciting poetry, you have to decide if you want to transform yourself into the newest shape and work toward becoming certified as a poetry-reciting widget-holder. If not, well, you're free to find something more challenging or satisfying to do.

What all that means to you is simple: You are in charge of your future. You may decide to continue your life within your current corporation. You may decide to look for another job. Or you may decide to become your own company, with or without employees of your own.

If you choose the last option, you'll have lots of company. The number of full-timers has now fallen below 70 percent of all American men. Of those employed, 25 percent are on a temporary, contract, or part-time basis (Economics Policy Institute in Washington, D.C.). According to the latest U.S. Bureau of Labor Statistics, about 10 million people are self-employed. Other private studies report almost 14 million self-employed (Find/SVP in New York and Link Resources Corporation, a New York-based subsidiary of International Data Group). The average tenure on a job, according to the latest figures from the U.S. Bureau of Labor Statistics, is 4.5 years.

You're at a major crossroads.

Whatever decision you make—even in a highly technical, fluctuating market with short-term jobs and short-term employees—you don't have to face a sour workplace. The Hay Group, a management consulting firm in Philadelphia, reported from its 1995–1996 employee attitudes survey that despite the ongoing downsizings, employees feel better about their jobs than they did just five years ago. Pride in one's company was high at all job levels.

You have two good choices: Be your own boss on your own payroll, or be your own boss on someone else's payroll.

## DEFINE SUCCESS IN YOUR OWN TERMS

Take your deliriously happy or decidedly disappointed condition and do some deep thinking. Define success in your own terms. As a professional speaker, I've made it a habit to collect definitions of success through the years. Here are a few you might find thought-provoking:

> Some men are successful for what they know, some for what they do, and a few for who they are.
>
> Success is the distance between one's origins and one's final destination.
>
> Success is having something to be enthusiastic about.
>
> He who has a talent and learns how to use it has won a triumph and glorious satisfaction few people will ever know.

Once you have defined success for yourself, you'll find decisions regarding job hunting, transfers, promotions, and entrepreneurial ventures much easier. If you're considering striking out on your own, talk with people who've done it (recently—not twenty years ago). If you're considering staying with your current employer and making yourself employable there regardless of what changes may come about, ask people who've made successful transfers of skills what it takes and if they'd do it all again. Plug their insights into your own evaluative questions:

- How much time do you want or need to spend with your family?
- How often do you see your friends? Is that important to you?
- What hours do you want to work?
- What opportunities do you have for personal growth?
- Do you like variety or routine in a job?
- How important—or unimportant—is it that your work has lasting value for humanity?
- What challenges will you face?
- Do you thrive on or become stressed with constantly changing challenges?
- Do you mind having other people (a boss or team leader) tell you what to do or veto your ideas?

- Do you enjoy working collaboratively with others (a boss, team leader, or coworkers)?
- Do you prefer to work alone?
- Do you mind moving to where the job goes?
- Would you like or hate to work from home?
- How much money do you need?
- How much money do you want?
- What is your greatest talent?
- What is the single most important thing in the world to you?
- What is the most important purpose or goal in your life?

Once you've determined your definition of success, you're ready for the next step.

## ASSESS YOUR STRENGTHS

If I asked you to pull out a sheet of paper and list ten skills, ten attitudes, and ten traits that would make you attractive to an employer or to a prospective customer or client wanting to buy your services, could you list these quickly? No, I'm not talking about technical skills like accounting, computer programming, or performing brain surgery. I'm talking about those generic skills, attitudes, and traits that win jobs and contracts—the second, third, and fourth times.

Computer languages will change. The need for mechanical or electrical engineers will expand and diminish. The tools for pancreatic surgery will become more complex or simpler. Technical specialties have become so narrow that an acquaintance of mine has a Ph.D. in food science, with a specialization in potatoes! The technical skills you'll need for a lifetime will be in constant flux.

Not too many decades ago, the average employee had 1.5 jobs during his or her lifetime. That means that half the people in the workforce worked for a single employer all their lives, and the other half of the employees worked for only two companies during their lifetimes. Now, according to research reported by Carole Hyatt in her book, *Lifetime Employability,* the average skilled person will probably have 10.5 jobs during a lifetime. On average, Americans have switched employers three times in the last ten years. Approximately one in 10 (12%) have changed occupations altogether, according to a Prudential Securities Jobs and Money Survey.

These jobs require basic (core) skills that, according to HR executives surveyed by Olsten Staffing Services, 26 percent of all new hires lack. But the core competencies won't change. In fact, the government gathered a rather impressive group of corporate CEOs in 1992 to head a major study to identify those core workplace competencies (the SCANS report). Few companies these days can guarantee you a lifetime job, but with core skills you can guarantee yourself lifetime employability. Organizations have decided that they're no longer paying for face time; they're paying for skills. And those skills are what this book's all about.

## USE THIS BOOK TO MAKE YOURSELF EMPLOYABLE FOR A LIFETIME

Life "happens" better with a plan. Here's how you can use and benefit from this book:

- You can increase your awareness of marketable skills and aptitudes—either as a full-time employee or an entrepreneur on your own—by reading the chapter headings and overview of each skill, trait, or attitude.
- You can assess your personal skills, attitudes, and values by completing the various "Rate Yourself" sections included with each chapter.

- You can formulate a self-development "master" plan from which you can set personal, self-improvement goals. (Consider it a second installment on Ben Franklin's idea.)
- You can identify suggestions for key points to include in your biography or resume submitted for freelance projects.
- You can gain pointers on items to highlight for your corporate performance reviews and discussions.
- You can select agenda items for mentoring/coaching activities.
- As a manager, you can provide this book to your employees as a blueprint for their career growth.

So, whether you're deliriously happy or decidedly disappointed, read on. As long as you have the prerequisite skills, attitudes, and traits to sell, you can thrive on change as a freelancer or as an employee. A career, not a job, gives you control.

*Dianna Booher*

# Career Fitness Inventory:

## Skills, Traits, and Attitudes That Make You Employable for a Lifetime

Review the following list and circle the appropriate number to assess your level of mastery of each skill, trait, or attitude. You may also want to make a copy of this checklist and ask your boss, spouse, and/or a coworker to record their observations of you and your work. Then use this "before" picture as a benchmark as you chart your progress toward personal career goals.

| | Novice | | | | | | | | Mastery |
|---|---|---|---|---|---|---|---|---|---|
| Discover Your Own Values and Define Success in Your Own Terms | 1 2 3 4 5 6 7 8 9 10 |
| Set Goals and Measure Achievements | 1 2 3 4 5 6 7 8 9 10 |
| Listen Effectively | 1 2 3 4 5 6 7 8 9 10 |
| Build Credibility and Rapport | 1 2 3 4 5 6 7 8 9 10 |
| Communicate Clearly One on One | 1 2 3 4 5 6 7 8 9 10 |
| Speak Before a Group with Authority and Confidence | 1 2 3 4 5 6 7 8 9 10 |
| Brief Others on Your Work and Situations | 1 2 3 4 5 6 7 8 9 10 |
| Write Clearly, Concisely, and Effectively | 1 2 3 4 5 6 7 8 9 10 |
| Edit Others' Writing | 1 2 3 4 5 6 7 8 9 10 |
| Read Widely and Stay Informed | 1 2 3 4 5 6 7 8 9 10 |

| | Novice | | | | | | | | | Mastery |
|---|---|---|---|---|---|---|---|---|---|---|
| Research Resources and Analyze Information | 1 | 2 | 3 | 4 | 5 | 6 | 7 | 8 | 9 | 10 |
| Interview Others to Gain Necessary Information | 1 | 2 | 3 | 4 | 5 | 6 | 7 | 8 | 9 | 10 |
| Develop a Recordkeeping System to Make Chaotic Information Usable | 1 | 2 | 3 | 4 | 5 | 6 | 7 | 8 | 9 | 10 |
| Organize Yourself, Workspace, and Tools | 1 | 2 | 3 | 4 | 5 | 6 | 7 | 8 | 9 | 10 |
| Manage Time Wisely | 1 | 2 | 3 | 4 | 5 | 6 | 7 | 8 | 9 | 10 |
| Travel Productively | 1 | 2 | 3 | 4 | 5 | 6 | 7 | 8 | 9 | 10 |
| Schedule Work Efficiently and Effectively | 1 | 2 | 3 | 4 | 5 | 6 | 7 | 8 | 9 | 10 |
| Plan Projects with Available Resources, within Budget, and on Schedule | 1 | 2 | 3 | 4 | 5 | 6 | 7 | 8 | 9 | 10 |
| Think Analytically: Inductive and Deductive Reasoning | 1 | 2 | 3 | 4 | 5 | 6 | 7 | 8 | 9 | 10 |
| Compute Numbers and Crunch Statistics So They Are Usable | 1 | 2 | 3 | 4 | 5 | 6 | 7 | 8 | 9 | 10 |
| Adopt an Entrepreneurial Spirit | 1 | 2 | 3 | 4 | 5 | 6 | 7 | 8 | 9 | 10 |
| Budget Appropriately | 1 | 2 | 3 | 4 | 5 | 6 | 7 | 8 | 9 | 10 |
| Understand Common Business Terms and Profitability Ratios | 1 | 2 | 3 | 4 | 5 | 6 | 7 | 8 | 9 | 10 |
| Lead Productive Meetings | 1 | 2 | 3 | 4 | 5 | 6 | 7 | 8 | 9 | 10 |
| Participate Actively in Meetings | 1 | 2 | 3 | 4 | 5 | 6 | 7 | 8 | 9 | 10 |
| Influence and Persuade Others | 1 | 2 | 3 | 4 | 5 | 6 | 7 | 8 | 9 | 10 |
| Negotiate Win–Win Outcomes | 1 | 2 | 3 | 4 | 5 | 6 | 7 | 8 | 9 | 10 |
| Mediate Conflicts of Others | 1 | 2 | 3 | 4 | 5 | 6 | 7 | 8 | 9 | 10 |

| | Novice | | | | | | Mastery | | | |
|---|---|---|---|---|---|---|---|---|---|---|
| Resolve Conflicts on Your Own | 1 | 2 | 3 | 4 | 5 | 6 | 7 | 8 | 9 | 10 |
| Solicit Usable Advice and Feedback | 1 | 2 | 3 | 4 | 5 | 6 | 7 | 8 | 9 | 10 |
| Admit Mistakes or Errors in Judgment | 1 | 2 | 3 | 4 | 5 | 6 | 7 | 8 | 9 | 10 |
| Be Receptive to Negative Feedback and Positive Suggestions | 1 | 2 | 3 | 4 | 5 | 6 | 7 | 8 | 9 | 10 |
| Give and Follow Clear Instructions | 1 | 2 | 3 | 4 | 5 | 6 | 7 | 8 | 9 | 10 |
| Delegate So Things Get Done Right | 1 | 2 | 3 | 4 | 5 | 6 | 7 | 8 | 9 | 10 |
| Appraise the Performance of Others | 1 | 2 | 3 | 4 | 5 | 6 | 7 | 8 | 9 | 10 |
| Coach Others to Success | 1 | 2 | 3 | 4 | 5 | 6 | 7 | 8 | 9 | 10 |
| Become a Leader | 1 | 2 | 3 | 4 | 5 | 6 | 7 | 8 | 9 | 10 |
| Be Resourceful | 1 | 2 | 3 | 4 | 5 | 6 | 7 | 8 | 9 | 10 |
| Practice Creativity | 1 | 2 | 3 | 4 | 5 | 6 | 7 | 8 | 9 | 10 |
| Exercise and Develop Your Memory | 1 | 2 | 3 | 4 | 5 | 6 | 7 | 8 | 9 | 10 |
| Motivate Others | 1 | 2 | 3 | 4 | 5 | 6 | 7 | 8 | 9 | 10 |
| Interact Productively with Others on a Team | 1 | 2 | 3 | 4 | 5 | 6 | 7 | 8 | 9 | 10 |
| Be Cooperative | 1 | 2 | 3 | 4 | 5 | 6 | 7 | 8 | 9 | 10 |
| Give Others Credit for Their Help | 1 | 2 | 3 | 4 | 5 | 6 | 7 | 8 | 9 | 10 |
| Understand the Value of Diversity | 1 | 2 | 3 | 4 | 5 | 6 | 7 | 8 | 9 | 10 |
| Be Humble about Your Skills and Achievements | 1 | 2 | 3 | 4 | 5 | 6 | 7 | 8 | 9 | 10 |
| Analyze and Learn from Failure; Be Teachable, Approachable, Coachable | 1 | 2 | 3 | 4 | 5 | 6 | 7 | 8 | 9 | 10 |

|  | Novice |  |  |  |  |  | Mastery |  |  |  |
|---|---|---|---|---|---|---|---|---|---|---|
| Be Punctual; Meet Deadlines | 1 | 2 | 3 | 4 | 5 | 6 | 7 | 8 | 9 | 10 |
| Be Positive and Pleasant; Show Enthusiasm and Drive | 1 | 2 | 3 | 4 | 5 | 6 | 7 | 8 | 9 | 10 |
| Solve Problems | 1 | 2 | 3 | 4 | 5 | 6 | 7 | 8 | 9 | 10 |
| Be Decisive | 1 | 2 | 3 | 4 | 5 | 6 | 7 | 8 | 9 | 10 |
| Make Quality Decisions | 1 | 2 | 3 | 4 | 5 | 6 | 7 | 8 | 9 | 10 |
| Apologize for Mistakes and Situations | 1 | 2 | 3 | 4 | 5 | 6 | 7 | 8 | 9 | 10 |
| Forgive and Refuse to Hold Grudges | 1 | 2 | 3 | 4 | 5 | 6 | 7 | 8 | 9 | 10 |
| Be Ethical and Do the Ethical Thing | 1 | 2 | 3 | 4 | 5 | 6 | 7 | 8 | 9 | 10 |
| Be Dependable | 1 | 2 | 3 | 4 | 5 | 6 | 7 | 8 | 9 | 10 |
| Take Initiative | 1 | 2 | 3 | 4 | 5 | 6 | 7 | 8 | 9 | 10 |
| Take Calculated Risks | 1 | 2 | 3 | 4 | 5 | 6 | 7 | 8 | 9 | 10 |
| Accept Ambiguity | 1 | 2 | 3 | 4 | 5 | 6 | 7 | 8 | 9 | 10 |
| Focus and Concentrate | 1 | 2 | 3 | 4 | 5 | 6 | 7 | 8 | 9 | 10 |
| Persevere | 1 | 2 | 3 | 4 | 5 | 6 | 7 | 8 | 9 | 10 |
| Accommodate Change; Be Flexible | 1 | 2 | 3 | 4 | 5 | 6 | 7 | 8 | 9 | 10 |
| Learn to Learn | 1 | 2 | 3 | 4 | 5 | 6 | 7 | 8 | 9 | 10 |
| Develop a Service Attitude | 1 | 2 | 3 | 4 | 5 | 6 | 7 | 8 | 9 | 10 |
| Nurture Personal Relationships | 1 | 2 | 3 | 4 | 5 | 6 | 7 | 8 | 9 | 10 |
| Practice Proper Etiquette | 1 | 2 | 3 | 4 | 5 | 6 | 7 | 8 | 9 | 10 |
| Maintain Emotional Equilibrium; Control Stress | 1 | 2 | 3 | 4 | 5 | 6 | 7 | 8 | 9 | 10 |
| Balance Personal, Family, and Business Priorities; Develop Your Spiritual Nature | 1 | 2 | 3 | 4 | 5 | 6 | 7 | 8 | 9 | 10 |
| Present Your Expertise Internally and Externally | 1 | 2 | 3 | 4 | 5 | 6 | 7 | 8 | 9 | 10 |

# I Make up the Rules As I Go Along

Discover Your Own Values and Define
Success in Your Own Terms

## The Skill, Trait, or Attitude

You know your own mind. You exhibit stability and have a sense of direction in knowing what you want in life and how to achieve it. You have carefully examined what's important to you and feel satisfaction in a job that allows you to pursue your important goals and feel successful. You have discovered a way to make a living while receiving deep fulfillment from your work.

## Uses on the Job

Accepting or turning down job offers or transfers

Delegating projects or accepting delegated projects

Receiving or rejecting training opportunities

Determining work hours and daily schedules

Spending your earnings and investing your money

## Run That by Me Again

Success can be measured in any number of ways: salary, title, prestigious employer, fame, pursuits that allow or encourage creativity, tasks that allow use of personal talents, control over your own destiny (where you live, how far you drive, what perks you enjoy), ample time to spend with family and friends, opportunity to work with a spouse or family member at the same job, community involvement, opportunities to contribute humanitarian service with life-or-death impact, service to God, or the greater good—whatever your beliefs are.

## So Why Should I Care?

Why should companies care that their employees discover their own values and find work that gives them personal satisfaction? Two reasons: The first issue revolves around money. It costs far too much (in dollars, time, and effort) to train an employee for job X, only to discover a year later that the employee doesn't like job X and wants to transfer to job Y.

The second reason that companies want to plug employees into the right slots concerns morale, passion, and productivity. Employees who enjoy their jobs and feel pride in them take "ownership" for seeing that the details get wrapped up, the quality stays in, and the mission is accomplished. Satisfied employees are generally productive employees. Unsatisfied employees are those who do just enough to get by until a better opportunity comes along.

Why should you yourself as an employee strive to keep redefining your values? For the same reasons. Working at something that you don't enjoy feels too much like hard work. On the other hand, working at something that you enjoy becomes play. When you enjoy your work, you delve into it with your heart, soul, and mind.

Doing unpleasant tasks ... for longer hours than you want ... with people you don't enjoy ... away from people who are important to you ... for purposes that don't matter to you ... puts you under mental, emotional, and physical stress. And that stress can kill you.

At the least, you may wake up one morning and realize that you've traded your life for dollars in a bank account, a riding lawn mower, a trip to Australia, a sports car, and membership in a health club. Make sure that the price has been right.

## So Show Me...

Jack Dreyfus, founder of the Dreyfus mutual fund, tells of his two lives in his book *The Lion of Wall Street*. One he lived as a savvy Wall Street financier and mutual fund manager, the other he lived as a humanitarian passionately trying to bring medical research and information to the American public. The philanthropic side of Jack Dreyfus's story began in 1958 when he found himself suffering from severe depression. He persuaded his doctor to prescribe phenytoin for him, a drug typically used to treat epilepsy, not depression. The drug returned him to good health almost overnight. After he learned of six other people with similar remarkable recoveries, he began a 40-year pursuit to bring the drug to the attention of the American consumer. He has established a charitable medical foundation, with the goal of making phenytoin available to people around the world. Jack Dreyfus is a man who has made both work and play of his passion.

People who can identify their values and passion so directly make excellent employers and employees. They change the world.

## Rate Yourself

Label each item according to its importance in determining your personal and career satisfaction:

**A** Most important
**B** Important
**C** Somewhat important
**D** Not important

Salary _____

Title _____

Prestigious employer _____

Prestige and fame _____

Pursuits that allow or encourage creativity _____

Tasks that allow use of personal talents _____

Control over my own destiny (where I live, how far I drive, daily schedule, number of hours worked each week) _____

Working with other people I like         _____

Ample time to spend with family or friends     _____

Opportunity to work with a spouse or family member at the same job     _____

Community involvement and service     _____

Opportunities to contribute humanitarian service     _____

Express service and devotion to God     _____

# I'm in It for the Long Haul

## Set Goals and Measure Achievements

### The Skill, Trait, or Attitude

Goal setting involves drawing a roadmap for a single project or a complete career journey. You visualize the outcomes you want and set deadlines to achieve them. Your goals are specific and measurable. For each goal, you develop an action plan and timetable to reach interim milestones. Periodically, you evaluate your progress and accordingly adjust your action plan, time frames, or goals to make sure you haven't changed you mind about the intended results.

### Uses on the Job

Developing a marketing brochure that generates 500 leads for your consulting service over the next two years

Designing a strategy to market product X and product Y on the Internet for a cost of under $20,000, with the long-term plan in place and the website designed within six months

Within the next year, learning to speak Russian fluently enough to translate business correspondence that comes into your office

Expanding your network of professional contacts by five people each month for the next year

Planning the annual associational meeting during July with an interesting enough program to generate attendance of at least 1,000 people

Gaining enough system programming experience to get approval on a transfer before December 1

Improving your oral presentation skills so that you generate at least ten invitations to speak at civic functions during the next two years

## So Why Should I Care?

People who don't set goals rarely go places—personally or professionally. Instead, they stall or stop. And people who don't seem to be going anywhere on the job lose interest and, consequently, the quality of their work eventually suffers.

Goalsetting, granted, takes guts. Some people refuse to set goals because they're afraid of failing. If they never set goals, they think they'll avoid failure, rejection, and criticism. Wrong. People who don't set goals just get rejected and criticized for lesser things.

Others fear to set goals because of the chaotic corporate pattern of endless restructuring. But instead of tossing goal setting to the wind, you have to build more flexibility into your career goals. Rather than setting a goal to be promoted to a specific job title, you may want to identify daily tasks that bring satisfaction and set as your goal getting a job that allows time for those activities.

Supervisors also gain great comfort and confidence in knowing that the people to whom they delegate projects understand what's involved in goal setting. They need to surround themselves with people who readily accept the challenge to "make things happen."

The higher you go in an organization, the more important goal setting becomes. Achieving a goal requires a higher order of commitment and skill than completing a task. People who don't set challenging goals for themselves, their staff, their department, or their organization will eventually find themselves relegated to doing only *tasks* or *jobs*. A goal, on the other hand, implies a mission, a destination, or results. And organizations pay for results.

## Rate Yourself

Write three career goals to achieve in the next 24 months. Be sure they're specific, measurable, and worthy of achieving.

1. _____

_____

2. _____

_____

3. _____

_____

# We Heard You, We Heard You, Already

Listen Effectively

## The Skill, Trait, or Attitude

You concentrate on listening to and interpreting spoken messages. You pay attention to the accompanying body language, tone of voice, inflection, and mood. You listen between the lines to what is not said as well as to what is said. You understand messages with attention to the speaker's purpose. You verify your understanding of the speaker's message by summarizing to him or her what's been said. Others feel understood when you listen.

## Uses on the Job

Listening to customers to match the right product to the right need

Listening to instructions to complete a task or learn a new skill

Listening to and advising a coworker about a problem

Listening to analyze information with which to make a decision

Listening to your staff to understand the severity of the problems they face or issues they need help with

Listening in a job interview to evaluate and hire the best candidate for a position

Listening to evaluate a job offer to determine how it fits your personal and career goals

Listening to evaluate people's emotional stability and the credibility of information they're providing

Listening to evaluate people's intentions or reasons for failure or success in order to discipline, coach, or reward them appropriately

## Run That by Me Again

Have you ever been riding along in your car, listening to the radio, when another passenger asks you,

> "Where did he say that accident was?"
>
> And you respond, "What accident?"
>
> "The eighteen-wheeler that jackknifed ... that's causing the pile-up?"
>
> "Oh, I guess I didn't hear that."

The DJ's traffic report slipped by you without grabbing your attention, yet you did hear the passenger friend who spoke to you. Such situations illustrate the difference between hearing and listening. Hearing is a passive activity. We hear sirens, printers, phones, and faxes, complaining coworkers, and cafeteria chitchat. But effective listening requires more—more attention and effort. Active listeners have to sort and file, interpret, evaluate critically to accept or reject, and offer appropriate feedback to the speaker.

## So Why Should I Care?

People who don't listen lose sales. People who don't listen fail to get the job. People who don't listen to their applicants, employees, and coworkers don't select the best people for projects and jobs. People who don't listen make poor decisions. People who don't listen miss deadlines. People who don't listen misinterpret others' reasoning and intentions. People who don't listen become embroiled in conflict. People who don't listen destroy relationships and fail to generate customer loyalty. People who don't listen to their markets don't stay in business.

## Tips

Make up your mind to listen. Stop what you're doing when someone speaks to you. Concentrate on what the speaker is saying.

Pay attention to a speaker's facial expression, body language, and voice inflection.

Evaluate the speaker's mood, timing, current situation, obvious agenda, and potential hidden agenda.

Don't discount what people say to you simply because you may not like them, respect them, know them, or consider them as well informed or educated as you are.

Consider your own receptivity: Do you listen for what you want to hear and refuse to listen to what you don't want to hear? What mood, frame of mind, or circumstance may affect your own interpretation? Who could provide a more objective interpretation of the message delivered to you?

## Rate Yourself

How often do family members say to you, "You're not listening to me"?

_____ Rarely     _____ Occasionally     _____ Often

How often do you have to ask for instructions or explanations more than once?

_____ Rarely     _____ Occasionally     _____ Often

Do coworkers and family members frequently seek you out for private discussions with the comment, "I've got a situation/problem—just wanted to sound you out on what I'm thinking and get your perspective"?

_____ Rarely     _____ Occasionally     _____ Often

Do people seem relieved, accepted, or appreciative after you've listened to them?

_____ Rarely     _____ Occasionally     _____ Often

# And If You Believe That, I've Got a Check for ...

Build Rapport and Credibility

## The Skill, Trait, or Attitude

To establish rapport means to build a harmonious relationship. Although all relationships don't necessarily imply friendship, you show respect for others and they, in turn, respect you. Credibility stems from rapport. Others feel that you respect them as individuals and they typically "cut you some slack" when problems arise. That is, they tend to believe the information you provide and attribute good intentions to you. Others like and trust you.

## Uses on the Job

Building rapport with customers so when you talk about your product or service they believe you

Persuading team members to go along with your recommendation or decision, even when they don't fully see things as you do in a particular situation

Generating action among employees or within a civic group to join a cause

Motivating others to cut expenses to avoid serious consequences

Inspiring others to take a risk and stretch their skills to reach a goal

Assuaging doubt when something or someone has raised questions about your competence, behavior, ethics, or intentions

Changing people's minds or feelings about a new policy or procedure

Encouraging people to risk money or effort

## So Why Should I Care?

Have you ever walked into a roomful of strangers and struck up a conversation with another individual on a relatively insignificant topic, and after five or ten minutes of conversation, walked away feeling that you'd known that person forever? In other words, something "clicked" between you. He likes fried frog legs and you like fried frog legs. She has triplets and you have triplets. His mother always nagged him about waiting to marry so late in life, and your mother always nags you for the same reason.

All those little commonalities are what give us an emotional connection to another individual in a relatively short time. The common but invisible bond that builds rapport between people may be similar values, goals, histories or experiences, likes or dislikes, personality quirks, family situations, education, or attitudes and philosophies about life and living.

When we think others are similar to us, we like them. When we like them, then we begin to make *big* assumptions—that we can trust what they say and do. Although sometimes the assumptions are invalid, these feelings make powerful connections—for managers, for salespeople, for leaders.

## Tips

Ask questions to learn more about other people and then listen to their answers.

Show respect, concern, and compassion for others. They'll be attracted by the attention.

Be genuine about your intentions when you share information or recommend actions.

Admit what you don't know, so people will believe you when you do claim to know.

Give complete, correct, current, clear information. Forget the psychobabble, industry babble, and technobabble. Shoot straight.

Don't exaggerate—unless people realize you're exaggerating to make a point.

Evaluate criticisms and objections; don't just discount people, dismiss what they say, or downplay your interest.

Be vulnerable. Don't be afraid to let people know you have weaknesses, personal feelings, concerns, worries, excitement, and passion about your work projects.

Dress to reflect the image you want to convey. If you look as though you slept under a bridge, people aren't going to be eager to follow your investment advice. On the other hand, if you're advocating servant leadership and austere budgets, forget the Gucci shoes and filet mignon luncheon served in your office.

## Rate Yourself

When you speak, do people typically

_____ Scowl?

_____ Smile?

_____ Look puzzled?

_____ Adopt the body language of a skeptic?

_____ Keep their distance emotionally and adopt a "wait and see" attitude before committing to action?

How often do you get invited to extracurricular events (baby showers, weddings, graduations, parties, celebrations) arranged by people with whom you work?

_____ Often     _____ Sometimes     _____ Rarely

Do you get accused or blamed for things for which you are not responsible?

_____ Often _____ Sometimes _____ Rarely

Do you find it easy or difficult to network among your work colleagues and in the community?

_____ Easy _____ Difficult

Do people seem to seek you out when they want "the truth"?

_____ Often _____ Sometimes _____ Rarely

# There's Just No Communication Around Here!

Communicate Clearly One on One

## The Skill, Trait, or Attitude

When communicating one on one, you organize and express your ideas and feelings so that others understand your point of view. You listen to others, reading the verbal and nonverbal cues to interpret messages accurately. They feel understood after talking with you. You give usable feedback to others and accept criticism without becoming defensive.

You give and accept praise freely. You ask appropriate questions and answer questions appropriately. You can say "no" or deliver bad-news messages without destroying a relationship and can apologize easily and appropriately. You negotiate situations and resolve conflict. You are aware of gender and cultural differences in communication styles.

## Uses on the Job

Engaging in conversations to establish relationships and build rapport with customers and coworkers

Advising others of your plans and goals and sharing information others need to do their job

Soliciting advice and feedback from a coworker or supervisor

Commending others for their work

Defending your rights without manipulating or offending others or responding to insensitivities or threats

Explaining decisions and actions or justifying them to key subordinates

## So Why Should I Care?

Good communication is much like breathing—when you're doing it right, no one notices. When you're having difficulty, relationships and projects come to a halt. All human relationships depend on communication. Your impression of other individuals (and theirs of you) typically rests on your various interactions with those people. From those interactions, you draw conclusions about how well they do their job and determine whether you'd like to become their friend.

Having an extroverted personality doesn't necessarily mean that someone has excellent communication skills. The best test of your communication skill is the responses you typically receive. Effective communicators routinely get positive responses and reactions from others.

In survey after survey among executives, managers, and human resource professionals, the two highest rated criteria for hiring decisions are attitude and communication skills.

## Tips

- Overview and then elaborate. Never give background information first. People will never understand your "background" until you state your point. Make your point, and then circle back and support it with any necessary detail.
- Have a sense of the dramatic when you talk. Consider the difference between having someone tell you about a movie they've seen or seeing the movie for yourself. We like "live" performances. Put action in the voice, face, body, and scene.Add a funny twist to the telling. Use description to set the scene. Add gestures and movement to

give the story or information a sense of action. Be energetic and animated.

- Match your tone to your intentions. Carefully consider your phrasing and inflection. Does your comment sound like you're accusing, blaming, appeasing, analyzing, or just plain leveling?

- When spoken to, respond rather than react. Reacting to someone's comment or a situation implies a knee-jerk response without thought for the impact. Responding, on the other hand, means a thoughtful, appropriate reply that most likely will have the impact you intend.

## Rate Yourself

Do you feel comfortable making small talk in a group of strangers?

_____ Often _____ Sometimes _____ Rarely

Do others seem to control, dominate, ignore, or even verbally abuse you?

_____ Often _____ Sometimes _____ Rarely

Do you work effectively with teams and other groups?

_____ Often _____ Sometimes _____ Rarely

Are you embroiled in ongoing conflict with others around you?

_____ Often _____ Sometimes _____ Rarely

Do you feel that what you have to say is important to others—do they pay attention when you speak?

_____ Often _____ Sometimes _____ Rarely

# So Just Give Us the Bottom Line

Speak Before a Group with Authority
and Confidence

## The Skill, Trait, or Attitude

You can organize your ideas and communicate oral messages appropriately to the intended audience and purpose: either to inform, to persuade, to train, to motivate, or to entertain. At your best, you select the appropriate audiovisual aids, articulate distinctly at the optimum speaking rate, and use vocal variety (tone, pitch, inflection, and volume). You can make a complex subject clear; inject energy and enthusiasm; use effective gestures and body language; add appropriate humor; respond to the audience feedback; field questions from the group; and appear relaxed, confident, and in control.

## Uses on the Job

Presenting information to staff, team members, or customers

Selling a product or service to a group

Soliciting funds from a group

Explaining a task, procedure, or project to a group

Making special event speeches (retirements, going away, promotions) for your staff or team members

Motivating your team to buy into a new goal or change

Responding to public inquiries and concerns about publicity in the press

Acting as a spokesperson during a crisis

Calling for group action or decision in a situation

Introducing another speaker to an audience

Moderating a panel or symposium

Running for public office

## So Why Should I Care?

If you do all your work behind closed doors and away from the scrutiny of others, your work and its value may go unnoticed. Some projects become valuable only when others learn about them. For example, if you identify a cure for cancer, you have to communicate that cure to others—either by speaking or writing—so that they can take advantage of and benefit from your discovery.

In addition to passing on needed information, there's another reason speaking skills are so crucial: Others, particularly supervisors, often judge your other skills by your speaking ability. Others only "see" what you're able to communicate to them.

When you hear a stranger's voice on the telephone, don't you form a mental picture of that person? Most people do. A deep, gravelly voice generates a picture of an authoritative person. A shrill, high-pitched, quivering voice hints of a young, timid caller. Those mental pictures may be totally incorrect, but such associations happen just the same.

Likewise, others often draw conclusions about your competence in other areas based on your speaking abilities. For example, as a bank loan officer, you may do a thorough risk analysis for a commercial loan, but if you present your conclusions to the loan review committee in a timid and nervous manner, they'll likely question your judgment and conclusions.

Your speaking skills generate either confidence or doubts about your work.

## Rate Yourself

Give yourself a score on the following items, which are all important when speaking before a group:

Attention-getting opening

Poor **1 2 3 4 5 6** Effective

Clear organization of key points

Poor **1 2 3 4 5 6** Effective

High-impact conclusion

Poor **1 2 3 4 5 6** Effective

Appropriate use of humor,
anecdotes, illustrations,
examples

Poor **1 2 3 4 5 6** Effective

Appropriate timing

Poor **1 2 3 4 5 6** Effective

Appropriate speaking rate

Poor **1 2 3 4 5 6** Effective

Vocal variety (volume,
inflection, pace)

Poor **1 2 3 4 5 6** Effective

Effective gestures and
body language

Poor **1 2 3 4 5 6** Effective

Use of movement and
space

Poor **1 2 3 4 5 6** Effective

High-impact visuals

Poor **1 2 3 4 5 6** Effective

Energy and enthusiasm

Poor **1 2 3 4 5 6** Effective

Relaxed, confident
manner

Poor **1 2 3 4 5 6** Effective

Effective responses
to questions

Poor **1 2 3 4 5 6** Effective

# So Here's What I'm up To

Brief Others on Your Work and Situations

## The Skill, Trait, or Attitude

Few projects get assigned and completed without having others eventually in the loop with you—customers, colleagues, or managers who have to approve, provide input, fund, or accept the work you do. You prepare to brief others on your work by determining others' primary interests and selecting the appropriate details to match those interests, by sorting the "nice-to-know" from the "need-to-know" facts, and by anticipating any probable negative reactions to your briefing. You organize and present your information and ideas in a logical, concise, clear, and understandable way. Playing the key role, you take charge of the briefing so that any next action is obvious and clear.

## Uses on the Job

Relating the results of a PR or marketing campaign

Reporting to an executive team about completed research

Presenting budget requests or justifying expenditures to your management team

Reporting findings and recommendations on a consulting project

Presenting accomplishments to your supervisor or team leader

Presenting the next step in a consulting project to your client, to gain approval to proceed to the next phase

Reporting actions taken by a subcommittee to your work team

Giving project updates when you meet your boss or coworkers at the water cooler

## So Why Should I Care?

If you can't tell others what you've been doing, what you're doing may be worthless. Rarely in today's team environment in the global economy do we have complete freedom to launch a project and see it through from start to finish without involving others in the process. For the most part, there are built-in checks with management or customers to make sure things are moving along as planned. Change happens quickly. The goals or guidelines may change while the project is underway.

Keeping others informed as you work also helps ensure their support—cooperation, funding, resources—and provides a safeguard that you stay on track all the way to the finish line.

You may be doing an excellent job on a project, but if you do it in a corner, you typically hit the wall sooner or later. Usually, the more vocal, the more visible. And the more visible, the more viable.

## Rate Yourself

Do people seem to understand the relevancy of the information you're presenting to them? Or, do they look at you with a "so what?" expression?

_____ Understand    _____ Look puzzled

When you give a briefing, do you frequently feel caught off guard with questions that you hadn't anticipated from others?

_____ Yes    _____ No

Do you routinely get your budget approved?

_____ Yes    _____ No

After a briefing, is your management or customer typically decisive about the next sign-off?

_____ Yes    _____ No

When you leave a briefing, is your *own* next step or action always clear?

_____ Yes _____ No

Are you getting more or fewer opportunities to brief others?

_____ More _____ Fewer

# I Read It, but I Didn't Know You Meant ...

Write Clearly, Concisely, and
Effectively

## The Skill, Trait, or Attitude

You communicate your ideas, information, directives, requests, and conclusions in written messages that others easily understand. You organize ideas or information well, selecting an appropriate structure and eye-appealing layout. You give careful attention to grammar and punctuation, word choice, detail selection, emphasis, persuasion, and accuracy of data. You can compose your thoughts from scratch without having a form or model document to copy. You revise and edit as necessary to make documents correct, clear, and concise. You write quickly and effectively.

## Uses on the Job

Writing memos, letters, reports, proposals, manuals, procedures, e-mail, directives, notes on daily work, budget justifications, research records, newsletters, specifications, advertisements, catalogs, marketing literature, product or service descriptions, legal briefs, contracts, press releases, annual reports

## Importance on the Job

Writing skills and speaking skills are the two most important skills in the typical employee's repertoire. Although most people speak more often than they write, well-written documents and e-mail messages have staying power and high impact. Here's why:

Buyers become bombarded with phone calls and face-to-face interruptions with people who "just want a word" with them. As a result, listeners often throw up a mental or emotional screen that deflects spoken messages. When people have too much noise coming at them in uncontrollable spurts, they refuse to take your message seriously.

Written messages, on the other hand, give the reader more control over the situation. A reader can review and ponder the information at leisure, verify it, consider the pros and cons, and prepare questions or responses that cut to the heart of the issues and cement a decision. Buyers of most big-ticket items and bosses considering recommendations from staff generally prefer to receive information in written form so they can give it deliberate thought before making a decision.

Written messages also build rapport with others, particularly when they are commendations of someone's work or expressions of appreciation. Because written messages represent more time and forethought than spoken messages, readers tend to appreciate the effort. "Staying in touch" notes often have a long-term payoff in increased business and stronger relationships.

Finally, written messages typically make things "official." You may make a loan agreement with the bank, receive a job offer for a whopping 25 percent salary increase, or accept a discount for early payment for a truckload of tires. But eventually someone will reduce the entire agreement to written words and even add a statement that says, in effect, "no oral agreements count—this written document is the whole deal."

So no matter how well you think and speak on your feet, eventually you have to translate most of your information, offers, ideas, or opinions to paper.

And that paper (your writing) has to be accurate. A missing or misplaced comma can totally reverse the meaning of a sentence. For example, consider these two sentences: "Please destroy the contracts which were sent to your office by mistake." (Meaning: Destroy the contracts that were sent by mistake, but we don't care what you do with the other contracts you received.) Or: "Please destroy

the contracts, which were sent to your office by mistake."
(Meaning: Destroy all the contracts; they were all sent by
mistake.) Meaning turns on the placement of a comma.

Although not always an accuracy issue, word choice
also has a great deal to do with reader receptivity. For example, consider positive and negative phrasing: "I can't
have that package to you until Thursday," versus "I can
have that package to you by Thursday."

Even a single word can persuade or antagonize a
reader. For example, consider the impact of the various
versions of the following comments to a customer:

"Your managers will save time using our Form 2666 to collect the product data," versus "Your managers must use
Form 2666 to collect the product data."

"We have designated a specific liaison, Margaret Salinas,
to handle your technical questions most efficiently," versus
"All of your questions must be routed through the designated liaison, Margaret Salinas, to ensure that our internal researchers do not duplicate their efforts in responding to your technical questions."

"I'm calling about your *late* payment," versus "I'm calling
about your *delinquent* payment."

Organization of ideas also contributes directly to the
clarity and impact of your message. Good writers summarize the message (findings, conclusions, opinions) up front
and then identify the next action to be taken. Then they
follow up that overview of the message and action with
supporting details and any necessary background to make
the message and action easier to understand.

Less skilled writers tend to think *as* they write. They
begin "in the beginning" with background information,
pile detail or fact upon detail or fact, and finally state their
conclusion or next action to be taken. If you want to test
the appropriateness of the structure of your documents,
watch someone read a document you've written. If he or
she has to read it twice to understand it, that's a good sign
the document is organized upside down.

You may sell yourself and your ideas orally in a meeting with a customer, client, or coworker, but generally more things get done more quickly when you put it in writing.

## Rate Yourself

Consider your typical memos, letters, reports, proposals, and e-mail messages as you respond to the following checklist:

What's your closing ratio on sales proposals? _____

What percent of your recommendations to your boss are accepted and acted upon? _____

How often do people call you for clarification on something you've written?

_____ Frequently _____ Occasionally _____ Rarely

Are you satisfied with how long it takes you to write a typical document?

_____ Yes _____ No

# I've Made a Few Editorial Comments—Hope You Won't Mind

Edit Others' Writing

## The Skill, Trait, or Attitude

Editing differs from writing in several ways: Writing involves the thinking process behind a document, as well as composing the document. As an editor, you do not superimpose your own style over the writer's style in an effort to rewrite.

Instead, you review a written document, marking unclear or grammatically incorrect phrasing. You raise questions about vague ideas, gaps in logic, and missing key points. You point out redundant ideas or circumlocutious phrases. You question the accuracy of facts and appropriateness of details. You verify with the author that the emphasis, tone, and conclusions of the writing convey what the writer intends. You know how to explain to writers how they can improve their writing so that it meets intended objectives. You refuse to rewrite, but instead coach others to rewrite.

## Uses on the Job

Reviewing a procedure that someone else has written and for which you have the technical expertise

Adding your input to a team project such as marketing literature

Supervising another employee who is compiling a report, letter, or memo that will be sent out over your signature

Proofreading a coworker's documents for accuracy and clarity

Reviewing and approving policy statements that will apply to your own staff and also to employees throughout the organization

## Run That by Me Again

The old saying that too many cooks spoil the broth definitely does **not** apply to writing and editing. The more people who review a document for accuracy, clarity, and completeness, the more likely it is that piece of writing will meet its intended purpose.

Why can't people edit their own work? For the same reason most people can't cut their own hair or pull their own teeth—they're too close to it. When a subject is too close to you, remembering what it was like not to know can be difficult. Only a fresh pair of eyes can review writing for the holes—gaps in logic, non sequiturs, missing details, redundant ideas, or ambiguous language.

A second reason editing our own work is difficult is internal voice inflection. When we edit, we tend to hear ourselves *saying* the words in our mind. We pause at the right spots and inflect the proper words. But the reader doesn't have that voice inflection. So what we think is on the paper often is not.

For the typical brochure that my company produces for marketing purposes, we hire an outside designer, graphic artist, and production liaison to work with the printer. Nevertheless, when the designer brings in the draft, we have eight pairs of eyes review it, not for typographical errors but for missing information, proper emphasis, appealing layout, accuracy, persuasiveness, ambiguity, and conciseness.

According to Ernest Hemingway, "Good writing is rewriting." Every writer needs a coach to lay the foundation for rewriting.

But that is not to say that rewriting encourages a team spirit. Few writers go in search of editors. Often, just the opposite is the case. People become as defensive about their writing as they are about their appearance.

So an editor must also use tact in identifying writing weaknesses and suggesting revisions. Editorial comments often involve subjective issues of personal preference and tone, and reviewers often find writers more accepting of comments framed as questions than absolute statements. For example, writers prefer "How about a table here to make this information more readable?" to "This is too confusing."

Finally, as an editor, remember to make positive as well as negative comments about the document. When something is well phrased, illustrated with the perfect analogy, or stated simply, clearly, and concisely, let the writer know. Editorial comments, whether positive or negative, give writers important feedback for their future work.

## Rate Yourself

Read the following poorly written passage, and see if you can identify specific weaknesses. Can you identify at least four specific things that need to be revised, and tell the writer why and how to improve them?

> Structured maps which have been contoured on the top of the Blaxton and San Matthews properties are shown in Figures 3A and 3B, respectively. Similarities exist between the structures of the two zones, with both being elongated carbonate buildups with the axes following an east-to-west direction. A determination should be made about who actually owns the properties. At the points of structural change, sections located in the lower parts of the San Matthews property can be said to become progressively less productive.

# Where Did You Read That?

Read Widely and Stay Informed

## The Skill, Trait, or Attitude

You read and interpret written information to do your job and stay current in your field: manuals, procedures, graphs, flowcharts, reports, proposals, specifications, announcements, studies, and journals. You grasp the main message and then locate the essential, pertinent details or data. You judge the accuracy or plausibility of what you read. You know when to read in detail, when to skim, and when to skip the reading altogether.

## Uses on the Job

Reading directions to assemble equipment

Learning a new software package

Reading a request for a proposal from a potential client and determining whether to take the time and exert the effort to prepare the proposal

Reading journals in a new industry to understand the mind-set and problems of potential customers so you can present your service to them more effectively

Reading specifications on a product from a manufacturer so that you can answer a buyer's questions

Reading a contract before signing it to make sure you can agree to all of its terms

Reading a management report so you can anticipate potential problems and take action before they become crises in your area of responsibility

## Tips

Don't read aimlessly. The time you spend reading meaningless, "nice-to-know" information may rob you of time to read the most essential information.

Read close to the event. There's no need to read a lengthy report that you'll not discuss with your team until four weeks later. Simply note on your calendar that the reading must be done and then read in depth immediately before the time you need to discuss the report. Then the facts will be fresh in your mind.

Make use of the summary blurbs provided with newsletter, journal, or magazine articles or the executive overview in internal reports. After reading the one- or two-sentence summary of the key points, do you need or want to know more? Nutshell versions may provide all the information you really need to stay informed.

Read the opening paragraph or two to get the main ideas. Make it a conscious decision whether to read further. Do you really need more detail?

Skim headings and first sentences of paragraphs for key points.

Focus on sidebar short takes that typically provide key facts, statistics, poll/survey results, or how-to's.

Read the captions under graphics; these should contain central, summary points or key details.

Pay attention to the subject lines in your e-mail messages.

Read selectively. Know when *not* to read by knowing why you're reading each piece in the first place. How do you plan to use the information?

## Rate Yourself

Do you attend meetings to discuss various reports and hear people bring up issues from the reading that you have missed or don't remember as essential?

_____ Frequently      _____ Sometimes      _____ Rarely

Do you read analytically? That is, do you question the veracity of the facts, polls, and conclusions presented in things you read?

_____ Frequently     _____ Sometimes     _____ Rarely

Do you have a backlog of reading material that's causing you stress?

_____ Frequently     _____ Sometimes     _____ Rarely

Do you feel informed and up to date about new trends in your field of expertise and in your industry?

_____ Frequently     _____ Sometimes     _____ Rarely

# I've Got More Information Than I Know What to Do With

Research Resources and Analyze
Information

## The Skill, Trait, or Attitude

You know where to find information and resources. You can assess the validity and value of information by researching its basis and source and comparing and contrasting it to other information available from other sources. Typically, you use the latest technology to access the most up-to-date research.

## Uses on the Job

Finding information about your competitors so you can keep your own services, policies, and prices competitive

Locating suppliers to provide the services or products you need

Determining the appropriate salary to offer a new employee hired in a new position

Analyzing the potential demand for a new service you want to provide

Reviewing completed research toward solving an ongoing problem that other organizations and industries have faced so that you can build on that research rather than duplicate it

Identifying gaps in the product or service offerings of your competitors

Determining preventative steps when you detect negative recurring trends

## So Why Should I Care?

Today, the question is not, "Do you know X?" The question is, "Do you know how to find out about X?" Mastery of a certain body of information is of limited value in a fast-moving workplace; what you know today may be wrong tomorrow. The real strength is in knowing how to access the latest information quickly and to verify its accuracy.

## So Show Me...

Current research has become an industry unto itself. Companies like Find/SVP, headquartered in New York City, have hundreds of employees on the phone daily to take caller questions about research not yet available in print form. Their sources? They call experts in the specifically related field and coax information from them to satisfy the queries of clients who absolutely must have the latest data and opinions. Here are a few examples of the research questions submitted to them:

A company wanted to find sponsors for "safe drinking" education and asked for a list of companies known for giving to causes unrelated to their core business. Find/SVP's list turned up Ben & Jerry's (peace), Visa (meals on wheels), and Nike and Benetton (racial harmony).

Another caller needed to have a list of people who had a color in their name (Red Skeleton, Shirley Temple Black).

A window manufacturer celebrating its 75th anniversary asked for a list of movies, books, songs, and fun facts that related to windows.

Find/SVP even has clients use their electronic brainstorming capabilities. The researcher posts a client's question on the internal e-mail. Within minutes, over 300 Find/SVP associates view the message and start sending their replies.

Electronic researching is in its infancy. The Internet, for example, has opened the door to unlimited research opportunities for the average person, researching on the job.

But a big challenge in analyzing information turned up by research is judging its validity. Consider the expert witnesses called on to testify in major criminal or civil court cases. Who is saying what, and who is paying them to say it? It's not—nor has it ever been—enough to know something; you must determine whether to believe something that is purported to be accurate and unbiased. As humorist Mark Twain once quoted Benjamin Disraeli: "There are three kinds of lies: lies, damned lies, and statistics."

Those who can research with a skeptical eye work best in our current environment.

## Rate Yourself

Would you know how to find the following information? Place a checkmark beside the items you would know how to research.

_____ The number of associations in the United States

_____ The president of Gulf Oil in 1978

_____ The copy machine with the fastest speed

_____ The number of single mothers in Russia

_____ The number of golfers over the age of 80

_____ The latest research findings on Alzheimer's disease

_____ The number of books in print on the subject of marketing

_____ The names of anti-virus software packages that are the most effective

_____ The most advanced procedures for emergency room care in the United States

_____ The names of competitors for specific customers

_____ The latest trends in your industry

_____ The number of in-person sales calls the average insurance salesperson makes each month

# So What You're Really Saying Is ...

Interview Others to Gain Information

## The Skill, Trait, or Attitude

Asking the right questions of the right people produces the right information. You know when and how to ask both open and closed questions to gain information or agreement. You understand that how you phrase the question drastically affects the answer you receive. You think quickly to interpret answers and follow up with additional probes to expand on the answers given.

## Uses on the Job

Investigating a complaint to resolve a customer satisfaction issue

Investigating an accident to determine its cause and identify preventative measures

Designing a questionnaire to survey employees or customers

Selecting the best candidate for a project or job

Interviewing potential clients to find ways your product or service could solve a problem for them, meet a need, or increase or improve their business

Interviewing a supervisor to gain appropriate information to complete a delegated project or to gain personal feedback on your performance

Interviewing people randomly to determine the viability of bringing a new product to market

Interviewing researchers to learn how their findings would apply to your own work

Interviewing potential employees to determine their suitability for various positions

**49**

- Ask open questions to gain information and expand your understanding. With an open question, you can probe for subjective feelings, invite interpretations, and uncover related issues that you didn't even know to ask about at the beginning. Open questions typically start with *how, what, why, to what extent, describe,* or *tell me more about.* Example: "What options do you think we should consider for financing the project?"

- Ask closed questions to gain agreement or narrow options. With a closed question, you can pinpoint specific details, probe for objective responses, and focus the discussion. Typically, closed questions start with *did, do, have, would, will you, can you, may, is, are, when, where,* or *who.* Examples: "Do you think Jana can handle this new PR campaign?" "Do you prefer to schedule the meeting after hours or during the normal workday?"

- Use probe questions like *what, why, when, where, how, how much?*

- Ask people their sources for data they provide or opinions they hold.

- Examine the phrasing of your questions for hidden biases that suggest to the other person what answer you want.

- Ask whimsical questions to learn more about a person's hopes, feelings, character, or goals. Example: "If you could have one year of paid leave to do anything you wanted, how would you spend your time?"

- Ask for ranges to gauge feelings about issues that people may hesitate to be specific about. Example: "On a scale of one to ten—one being 'no way can we pull this off' and ten being 'I've already decided how to spend the bonus'— how do you feel about your chances for meeting the quota on this new product?"

- Watch for phrasing and a tone of voice that makes the other person feel defensive or threatened.

- Listen, really listen, to the answers you receive.
- Remember that "A prudent question is one half of wisdom," according to Francis Bacon.

## Rate Yourself

Write two open questions that would have helped you to understand the last project you were delegated.

1. _____
2. _____

Write two closed questions that would entice someone to agree with you about an issue.

1. _____
2. _____

Do coworkers often ask you to talk to someone (interview a job applicant, visit with a potential vendor, solve a customer problem) to help them make a decision?

_____ Frequently _____ Sometimes _____ Rarely

How many hiring mistakes and successes have you experienced?

| As Interviewer | As Interviewee |
|---|---|
| _____ Successes | _____ Successes |
| _____ Failures | _____ Failures |

# I Think I Read Something on That a While Back

Develop a Recordkeeping System to Make Chaotic Information Usable

## The Skill, Trait, or Attitude

You have a system for filtering information hurdled at you and logging it in (metaphorically speaking) so you can retrieve it and massage it when necessary. Your workspace functions as an organized center for paperwork that needs your attention.

You know how to recover articles, information, and statistics from your professional publications that can be useful to you in doing your job. You can quickly locate vital information for your personal life and your job. You do not become easily distracted by the unnecessary information that comes your way. You ignore or discard the inappropriate and focus on storing only information that will be useful for later reference.

## Uses on the Job

- Gathering industry news and trends that affect the way you make, sell, or service your product
- Collecting statistics for a speech to your community or coworkers to motivate them to contact their representatives in Congress about a political issue
- Writing a report or proposal to substantiate a new trend upon which your company should base future products or services

- Persuading a customer to buy by providing information pertinent to his or her situation

## So Why Should I Care?

The total body of information now doubles every seven years. Database management software has become a ubiquitous computer tool precisely because of the need to handle so much random information arriving at an alarming pace: catalog numbers and quantities of items in your warehouse, your competitors' pricing information, possible vendors for the latest technology in your industry, customer preferences, fax and phone numbers.

For those hard copy items that you can't or don't want to enter into your computer memory, we have to contend with paper files. Records management experts tell us that we misfile three percent of the items that we actually keep. How many minutes each week do you spend looking for misplaced information? Can you afford that kind of time? Can you afford to lose key information? Having information "somewhere" is useless if you can't find it when you need it.

Being able to locate facts quickly also makes a positive impression on clients. The days of mass marketing are fast coming to an end. Clients want customized, not generic, solutions. Therefore, they expect you to customize your presentations to them as well. If they take the time to pull three or four people off the job to meet with you to help you understand their company, they expect your proposal and work for them to incorporate the information they've given you.

## Rate Yourself

Where would you file or retain the following tidbits of information? Suggest an appropriate category for each item.

National survey results offering salary information on people in your occupation

Literature and pricing information on a competitor's product

Instructions for operating and maintaining a new household gadget

A cartoon you may want to use in your next staff meeting

A statistic for an upcoming oral presentation

An intriguing investment strategy and accompanying computations on tax-free investments

Articles about changes coming to your industry

An overheard comment about a possible merger involving your primary competitor

A pocket-size guide for tipping while traveling in foreign countries

# It's Here Somewhere—Just Give Me a Minute

Organize Your Self, Workspace, and Tools

## The Skill, Trait, or Attitude

You organize your schedule to minimize time crunches. You design your workspace, information, and tools so that you can work most efficiently without delays and interruptions caused by disorganization.

## Uses on the Job

Organizing workspace and tools to complete a project

Organizing a warehouse or inventory of a product or equipment

Creating a filing system

## So Why Should I Care?

Here's what others think when they see a disorganized workspace:

- He's obviously disorganized and incompetent.
- She can't determine priorities; therefore, I'd better not trust her to meet a deadline.
- He isn't focused; no wonder we get such fuzzy directives and policy statements.
- She is trying to look important with all these paperwork piles; I bet most of it is "grunt work" that somebody else should be doing.
- The desks of senior executives don't look like this. Who's he trying to kid?

- She can't handle the job; otherwise, why would there be such a paperwork pileup and bottleneck?
- He can't trust others. Why else would they all have to prepare so many reports and memos to keep him informed?
- It's a cinch she doesn't pay her bills on time.
- I wonder if his whole life is this out of control.
- I don't want to route anything to her for approval or input. That'll only mean a delay.

## Tips

- Keep only one, up-to-date calendar for both personal and work use.
- Keep your desk gadgets and tools in their appropriate places, which should be within easy reach as you work.
- Put pending items in a pending file or stack box after logging them onto your to-do list or calendar.
- Label things before you toss them somewhere.
- For paper items that you can't handle completely because you're waiting for information, approval, or input, add a post-it note at the top, stating what you're waiting for and the next action to be taken. Don't make yourself re-read the entire paper to remember what you planned to do with it next.
- When gadgets don't work, repair them or discard them. Don't extend their lives on your desktop, shelf, or workspace.
- Keep your filing up to date.
- Purge files periodically so you don't have to look through so many items to find what you need.
- Use "destroy" dates on items you file or pile. With destroy dates, anyone who encounters something after the destroy date has passed is at liberty to discard it without further investigation. Otherwise, things clutter up space indefinitely.

- Toss out unread journals, magazines, or newsletters more than three months old.

## Rate Yourself

Do you have to move away from your workspace to find "room to work"?

_____ A problem  _____ Under control

Do you spend more than 10 minutes a week looking for lost items?

_____ A problem  _____ Under control

If you were in the hospital, could you tell someone exactly where to find items or information to take care of your job in your absence?

_____ A problem  _____ Under control

Do you get stressed just looking at your desk?

_____ A problem  _____ Under control

# Is It Already Six O'clock?

Manage Time Wisely

## The Skill, Trait, or Attitude

You make the best use of your time to meet your intended goals and assignments. You rank activities in order of importance, allocate the appropriate time to complete them, and plan and follow your work schedule. You recognize and minimize time wasters in your work day.

## Uses on the Job

Meeting a client's deadline for a proposal or project

Handling internally assigned projects to meet deadlines

Making yourself available to staff or team members as a leader or resource

Completing work activities within the normal workday so that you have time left for other non-work-related activities in your life

## So Why Should I Care?

Time is money. The triteness of the statement doesn't make it less true. In today's economy, minutes and dollars carry equal weight in work decisions big and small.

For example, consider the decision regarding starting salary for a new employee. Nina has been out of the workforce for eight years and interviews for a position as office manager. She explains that she has not kept up with the latest technology in the industry and will need time to reacquaint herself with the various software packages and applications in the new office. Let's say the employer had intended to pay a starting salary of $45,000 for an experienced person. If Nina convinces him she can do the job, the employer may offer her the job, but reduce the starting salary accordingly. He will calculate four weeks for learning time and compute the time lost before she's up to speed ($865 weekly salary × 4 weeks = $3,462). The employer will probably subtract the learning time and offer Nina a salary of $41,500. Time equates to hard dollars.

The same is true in purchasing decisions. Recently, our company evaluated bids from builders to construct a new office building in the Dallas-Fort Worth metroplex. The winning bidder's quotation came in at 16 percent higher than the next bidder. So why did we select that builder? After all the reference checks and inspections for quality, it came down to a decision based on time and deadlines. The highest bidder had a solid reputation from his past clients for meeting projected completion dates. When we factored in "what if's" concerning the other bidders' history in not meeting deadlines, we simply did the calculations. Paying even two more lease payments to stay in the leased space our company then occupied would have cost more than the 16 percent difference. Once again, time equates to hard dollars.

Someone who mismanages time costs the company money, not to mention headaches.

## Rate Yourself

|  | Satis-factory | Need Improve-ment | I'm Desperate |
|---|---|---|---|
| I use quick, informal techniques for communicating. | _____ | _____ | _____ |
| I know when to talk and when to write. | _____ | _____ | _____ |

| | Satis-factory | Need Improve-ment | I'm Desperate |
|---|---|---|---|
| I look for ways to reduce paperwork and streamline processes for myself and others. | _____ | _____ | _____ |
| I typically feel caught up on my work at the end of each month. | _____ | _____ | _____ |
| I do not allow unplanned interruptions to waste my time. | _____ | _____ | _____ |
| I plan my work and work my plan. Rarely do I get trapped in crisis situations. | _____ | _____ | _____ |
| Others frequently comment on how productive I am. | _____ | _____ | _____ |
| If my company paid for productivity alone, I would make an excellent salary. | _____ | _____ | _____ |

# Ticket, Please?

Travel Productively

## The Skill, Trait, or Attitude

You make optimum use of travel time by scheduling suitable work tasks to be done on the road: during air flights, waiting time between appointments, long trips across the city by car or mass transit. You also make travel time productive by piggybacking trips to accomplish multiple objectives.

## Uses on the Job

Traveling to company meetings and conventions

Traveling on client business

Traveling to sell to prospects and clients

Traveling to participate in or conduct training programs

Traveling to attend industry functions

Traveling to troubleshoot problems in your own company

## So Why Should I Care?

The information highway has not yet made business travel obsolete. According to the latest available Survey of Business Travelers sponsored by the Official Airline Guide and the Travel Industry Association of America, 38.4 million U.S. adults took 220 million business trips in 1994. That's a lot of salary sitting on a plane or in a car for an extended time.

It's not unusual for some professionals to spend one-third to one-half of their time on the road. For the $60,000 employee, that means the company is staking $30,000 on the wise use of travel time.

## Tips

- Schedule flights for off-peak hours (lower costs, less chance for delays and missed connections, less stress, fewer travelers, and more room to spread out to work).
- Schedule direct flights when possible to reduce total travel time and chance for delays and missed connections.
- Use travel time for brain projects: thinking about options for solving a problem, analyzing a decision, planning.
- Carry a reading file of reports, newsletters, journal articles, and other items that have no certain deadline.
- Return your phone calls from the road; don't wait until you have six hours' worth of calls back in the office.
- Travel with your computer and send e-mail responses to those who need immediate answers.
- Prefer room service for meals to gain uninterrupted work time in the evenings.
- Keep a bag packed with duplicate items such as toiletries, makeup, exercise clothes, robes, and so forth.
- Schedule your meetings on the road as carefully and closely as you would schedule them in your home city. As you set appointments, ask for information about distance and travel time between appointment locations.
- Travel with the basic office necessities such as paper clips, post-it notes, stapler, calculator, calendars, and so forth.

## Rate Yourself

Does your absence from the office delay others waiting on your approval or input for their projects?

_____ Yes    _____ No

Do you feel "tied to your office" for *real* work because you're not equipped or prepared psychologically or physically to work on the road?

_____ Yes    _____ No

Can you pack for a three-day trip in 10 minutes or less?

_____ Yes    _____ No

Do you frequently feel stressed out and behind from routine travel?

_____ Yes    _____ No

# A Few Minutes Here, a Few Minutes There ... and Pretty Soon It's a Total Mess

Schedule Work Efficiently and Effectively

### The Skill, Trait, or Attitude

Scheduling your work means having a clear picture of your overall responsibilities and what importance each has to your overall success. With this understanding, you set priorities for tasks and plan your days and weeks with those priorities in mind. You understand how different responsibilities and demands overlap. You understand the importance of constantly reviewing priorities and revising your scheduled activities.

### Uses on the Job

Telling customers when you'll get back to them with answers, quotations, or proposals

Meeting project deadlines set by your own management

Scheduling your typical workday and workweek

### So Why Should I Care?

I recently remarked to a friend that his title on his new business card was not one I'd seen before and asked him to elaborate on his responsibilities. He responded, "I haven't figured all of them out yet. I'm inventing my job as I go along. Basically, I was hired to make sure we have capable people to move into the top slots when our executives retire. It'll take me a year or so to figure out exactly how I'm going to do that and what my typical week will look like."

That's becoming a more typical scenario in today's fast-changing workforce. Twenty years ago, an employer told you what job to do—and often, how to do it. Not so today. With empowered individuals in flat organizations with quick access to the latest information and technology, people have freedom to decide what to do, how to do it, and when to do it.

## So Show Me...

After you decide what to do, you need to know how to get it on your calendar and get it finished. Several years ago, I was in Oregon meeting with a husband and wife executive team. When we began to try to schedule our next meeting, the husband and wife both pulled out their Day-Timers. This conversation followed:

> Dave said, "How about our coming to Dallas again on Thursday and Friday two weeks from now?"
>
> Katlin responded: "Wait, that won't work for me. I'll be finalizing the new pricing structures and policies for our overseas distributors."
>
> "But that can wait, can't it? You're not meeting with any of the distributors, are you?"
>
> "No, but I told them I'd have the information ready the following Monday. So I'll need Thursday and Friday to put things together and review it with our people here."
>
> "You mean you actually have that scheduled—written down—on your calendar?" Dave looked incredulous.
>
> "Of course. How else would it get done if I didn't schedule it?"
>
> Dave shrugged, acquiesced, and glanced in my direction. "Maybe that's why she meets her deadlines and I don't."

Although I had bowed out of the husband-wife conversation, Dave had just stumbled onto a simple principle of personal scheduling. If something is important enough to get done, it deserves a place on the work calendar. That doesn't mean that you can plan every hour of your day. On the contrary, you need to leave adequate space for unplanned events and demands. But you do need to schedule work time for important projects so they have your full attention.

The difference between a scheduled day and an unscheduled day is the stress level and the sense of accomplishment you feel when you leave the office.

## Rate Yourself

What's your record in meeting deadlines?

_____ Always     _____ 50/50     _____ A few

How often have scheduling, planning, and deadlines become the subject of negative discussions in your performance reviews?

_____ Often     _____ Occasionally     _____ Never

Do you end your typical week with a sense of accomplishment, or a feeling of frustration at not completing what you had intended to?

_____ Accomplishment     _____ Frustration

# If It Happens, It Happens

Plan Projects with Available Resources, within Budget, and on Schedule

## The Skill, Trait, or Attitude

To plan a project, you identify the ultimate objective and then decide what needs to be done to achieve that objective. Those actions or steps may be part of one big project or a series of smaller projects to achieve the bigger goal. After identifying the actions or projects, you determine the schedule or timetable for each step, who is accountable for each step, and the resources (money, people, information) you have available to complete the project. You also determine ways to get feedback to make sure you're on target along the way and to evaluate your results upon completion.

## Uses on the Job

Planning a marketing campaign
Developing a new product or service
Writing a policy manual
Converting all computer applications to a new platform
Developing a client proposal
Conducting an employee survey and reporting results
Designing and developing a new employee training course
Redesigning the building lobby
Staffing for a new project

## Tips

As a planner, you can't hide away in your office and move things and people around on a model or a computer screen. The difference between planning a project and carrying out a project—on time and within budget—can be enormous. Consider the following tips as precautions to see that things happen as you plan them:

- Be persuasive when you present your plans. It's not enough to be logical and factual. Others, such as bosses, accountants, and staffers, need motivation and conviction that what you envision will really happen.

- Respect the interim deadlines and target dates throughout the process. Otherwise, by example, you'll train others involved in the project that the deadlines are not to be taken seriously "as long as we get it done in the end." A client of mine, who was my liaison for a quarter-million dollar project last year, asked me to put together a timetable for a customer service project. She wanted the list of steps and corresponding deadlines. When I told her I wasn't far enough along in researching and planning the project to commit to deadlines yet, she said, "Oh, just take a guess; our company never pays any attention to deadlines anyway. We expect things to be late."

- Include others who will help you carry out the project in the planning phase. Otherwise, if you don't have their buy-in, your project may be a target for sabotage.

- Execute your plans with a sharp eye. Continually keep this question in the back of your mind: "Is there a way to do this cheaper, better, faster?"

## Rate Yourself

List your last five projects below. Then evaluate your planning skills by checking the boxes beside each:

|  | Met Deadlines | Within Budget | Achieved Objective |
|---|---|---|---|
| 1. _____ | ☐ | ☐ | ☐ |
| 2. _____ | ☐ | ☐ | ☐ |
| 3. _____ | ☐ | ☐ | ☐ |
| 4. _____ | ☐ | ☐ | ☐ |
| 5. _____ | ☐ | ☐ | ☐ |

# There's Gotta' Be a Better Way

Develop Systems and Procedures

## The Skill, Trait, or Attitude

Systems and procedures keep you from reinventing the wheel on your job. As a systems thinker, you automatically develop an overview of a job to be done and begin to conceptualize and experiment with how to do it most effectively. Once you discover the best system, you understand the value of recording the steps so that it becomes a repeatable process for the next time or next person.

## Uses on the Job

Developing a system for receiving customer feedback on an ongoing basis

Setting up a filing system for your office

Compiling boilerplate passages to include in customer letters or proposals and keeping the most current version accessible by all your field salespeople

Determining a process for keeping track of incoming calls and monitoring the workload of the people staffing the phones

Handling convention registrations from around the world delivered by phone, fax, mail, and e-mail

Setting up a system to collect and deliver mail throughout your organization

Determining how to handle travel arrangements for all the consultants in your department to ensure they book the most direct, economical route for client projects and that the expenses are charged back to the appropriate client

Creating a procedure to orient new employees

**69**

## Elaboration

Lack of conceptualizing in systems causes headaches: "The left hand doesn't know what the right hand is doing around here!" was probably first uttered in frustration over lack of a standard procedure. How do you know if chaos is creeping into your work group? Comments such as these indicate trouble:

Did you call the client? I thought I was supposed to call the clients.

Did you already pull that file? I thought we kept a record of those transactions on the computer?

You just finished all the calculations? So why did my boss ask me to do the same computations?

Is this manual put together right? Don't we have a model somewhere to refer to?

Who authorized this payment? All those bills are supposed to come through me!

I just transferred into this department—you guys certainly do things differently here.

Oh, was I supposed to do that? Doesn't Sonya usually handle that?

Any of these situations could indicate either that there are no systems in place or that people don't understand the systems or procedures. The result: duplicated effort, things that fall through the cracks and don't get done, turf wars, poor customer service, relearning ad infinitum, frustration, and careless control over money. In short, bad business.

## Rate Yourself

Could you pick up a piece of routine paper or a typical form in your office and trace where it came from and why, and where it goes when it leaves your department and why?

_____ Yes    _____ No

Name any four processes in your area of responsibility:

1. _____    3. _____

2. _____    4. _____

Do you routinely create this-is-how-we-did-it records when you complete a project so that you can handle the next similar task faster and easier?

_____ Yes    _____ No

Do you have a standard procedure for cleaning your house, apartment, or garage?

_____ Yes    _____ No

# *Where Did You Come up with That Idea?*

Think Analytically: Inductive and Deductive Reasoning

## *The Skill, Trait, or Attitude*

You can discover an underlying relationship between facts, objects, events, situations, or written passages and draw a general conclusion (inductive reasoning). Conversely, you can take a general conclusion or principle and apply it to understand a specific new situation or solve a specific new problem (deductive reasoning).

## *Uses on the Job*

- Reviewing the amount of money spent on advertising, and tallying the number of leads generated and products sold to determine where best to spend future advertising dollars

- Investigating the last 10 on-the-job accidents and devising a set of preventative measures for all employees to follow

- Interviewing an applicant about the last five positions she has held to determine if she will be a suitable match for the new job opening

- Reviewing bids from five potential suppliers to select the one most likely to do the best job for you

- Reading journals and newsletters from different industries to determine if the way companies in those industries are finding new markets could apply to locating new markets for your own products

- Listening to testimonials from satisfied customers interviewed on television about good customer service from Company A and identifying ways to improve your own customer service department
- Inspecting products on the market similar to yours to determine if your competing product is priced appropriately
- Reading economic reports to determine how best to invest excess cash
- Intercepting a call from an angry coworker in your boss's absence and deciding whether to return the call immediately yourself or leave the call until your boss returns

## So Why Should I Care?

IBM chief Louis Gerstner was quoted in *Time* magazine about the need for thinking workers: "What is killing us is having to teach them to read, compute ... and to think."

To think or not to think—that's **not** the question. There are people who can formulate theories but can't draw conclusions from evidence, and there are people who can draw conclusions but can't formulate specific guidelines for the future. Neither represents critical thinking on the job. Instead, on-the-job success comes from applying that thinking to some practical end in a real situation.

For example, an inductive-reasoning salesperson may lose five straight sales deals and draw an accurate conclusion about why she lost the sales. But if she can't take that conclusion and then figure out how to present her products to her customers in a more persuasive way or how to find more qualified customers, she won't improve her sales.

Likewise, a deductive-reasoning recruiter may understand that people who say they like to travel for leisure don't necessarily enjoy business travel. But if the recruiter can't interview applicant Hank about his travel preferences and limitations and determine whether he's going to be a good traveling salesperson, then the recruiter most likely won't make a good hiring decision.

The point is simple: Reasoning skills need to be tied to a real situation to pay off. Knowing all the answers doesn't do you any good unless you can match the right answers with the right questions.

## Tips

- Don't let sloppy language—yours or someone else's—get in the way of clear thinking: ambiguous meanings or labels reflecting judgment rather than evidence.
- Separate fact from opinion about a situation.
- Avoid letting your emotions overcome your logic. We are all particularly susceptible to heated personal attacks, flattery, appeals to our sympathy, or appeals to our power.
- Be aware of when you might be starting with a bias and looking for information to support that bias.
- Be careful about reasoning in the path of least resistance: We solve a problem in a certain way or make a certain decision because we've always solved the problem that way or always made that specific decision. Examples: We always buy a Buick. We always stay in a hotel in downtown Chicago. We always hire MBAs as operations managers.
- Resist the pull of testimonials—making a certain choice because someone more famous or powerful says it's the right decision.
- Don't give in to your gut. Intuitive thinkers "reason" on the basis of what feels right, on hunches. Hunches may or may not be based on applicable subconscious information.
- Saturate your mind with information about the situation so your reasoning mind has ammunition to work with.

## Rate Yourself

Do you find it easy to analyze the truth or error in newspaper editorials?

_____ Yes _____ No

Do you examine questionnaires or surveys to determine their validity for gathering objective information?

_____ Yes _____ No

Do you analyze why someone does something out of character in a particular situation?

_____ Yes _____ No

How often are you aware of your own motivations for decisions and actions?

_____ Often _____ Sometimes _____ Rarely

# This Checkbook Is Not Exactly Rocket Science

Compute Numbers and Crunch Statistics
So They're Usable

## The Skill, Trait, or Attitude

You can add, subtract, multiply, and divide—and know when to do which. You understand numerical concepts such as calculating with whole numbers and finding percentages. You can use a calculator and spreadsheet. You can review tables, graphics, and charts to gather or present quantitative information. Using mathematical computations, you can solve real-world problems and make real-world decisions.

## Uses on the Job

Calculating what percentage of your sales leads actually turn into sales

Solving a system of linear equations to calculate your business break-even point on a new product line

Given the half-life of a radioactive substance, determining how long nuclear wastes must be stored before the amount of radioactivity is negligible

Verifying the accuracy of your commission check, based on different commission percentages for each product sold

Calculating how many times you need to turn over your inventory to meet your financial projections for the year

Planning meal portions to serve to hospital patients to meet the prescribed nutritional requirements (such as proteins, vitamins, calories)

Given the pitch of a roof, determining the length of the beams needed for construction of a warehouse

Given the speed of oil flowing through a pipeline, determining how many hours it will take the oil to reach its destination

Reviewing a graph presenting the number of employees in Company X who have accepted an early retirement package; applying the percentages and compensation packages to your own organization to determine how many employees will likely accept your similar package

Reviewing your expenses on a specific 18-month project to determine how your actual expenses compare to your forecast expenses

Mixing a chemical formula for a new product; recording and reporting the changes in porosity as you increase the amount of a certain chemical in the formula

Computing your profit margin to determine volume discounts to offer a customer

## So Why Should I Care?

Numbers, statistics, and money make the world go around. If you don't believe it, flip through any current magazine or journal and look at the published numbers in surveys, graphs, charts, and other sidebars of information. Mathematical comparisons provide one of the most accessible ways to transfer concepts from one company to another and from one industry to another.

The tiniest numerical mistakes do cost billions. A decimal point moved one digit to the right or left in a sales contract could bankrupt an organization.

One of my recent clients is a national automobile manufacturer. During my observation process in customizing a customer service training program for them, I was shocked at how many customers had no concept of how much interest they were paying on their car loans. They were completely at the mercy of the automobile dealership to calculate their payments and apply any extra principal payments correctly. Still fewer customers had any idea how to determine whether buying or leasing a car served their financial situations more appropriately. They were at the mercy of their accountants or the dealership to tell them whether leasing or buying a car was more favorable to their tax situations.

Mathematical processes provide the platform for problem-solving and decision-making skills. In short, mathematical concepts and skills provide the most essential information for launching and operating a successful business or surviving as a consumer.

## Rate Yourself

If you're applying for a $240,000 bank loan at nine percent interest and the loan officer tells you that the conversion factor to determine your monthly payments is 10.35 per $1,000 of loan balance, what would be the amount of your monthly payment? _____

If your office is 11 feet by 14 feet and the unit price per square yard of the carpet you've selected is $18.99, how much will it cost to recarpet your office? _____

Do you find mathematical teasers intriguing or frustrating?

_____ Intriguing     _____ Frustrating

If you lost your handheld calculator and couldn't activate your computer spreadsheet, would you be able to prepare your budget report with a pen and paper?

_____ Yes     _____ No

# I'm the Best Boss I'll Ever Have

Adopt an Entrepreneurial
Spirit

## The Skill, Trait, or Attitude

Entrepreneurialism involves recognizing the business opportunity and taking a risk appropriate to that opportunity. You make decisions with the same care that you would use in running your own business. You consistently examine operations to find ways to cut costs and improve productivity. Innovative ideas get your attention. You search for ways to add value for both your internal and external customers. You understand that your contribution to the organization must outweigh your cost (salary).

## Uses on the Job

Suggesting a new way to measure customer satisfaction and improve your customer ratings

Recommending elimination of a redundant task in processing orders

Asking the powers that be *why* when you don't understand the necessity of a process and suggesting a faster way to accomplish the same goal

Circulating a journal article to your boss, and explaining how an idea in another industry might be translated to your own industry

Deciding about the wisdom of giving a potential customer a volume discount for a large multi-year contract

Turning down business that's only marginally profitable because of the lost opportunity to use your production team for a larger project

## So Why Should I Care?

In flat organizations with so many people reporting to fewer executives, employees have to be their own supervisors on a day-to-day basis. They have to take initiative in seeing how to improve the business rather than waiting for the boss to tell them which tasks to accomplish first and how to do the job.

The easiest employees to supervise are those who think like independent contractors. That is, they have to build their own credibility for consistent performance, they have to prove their value to the company, and they have to please their customers—the people who sign their paychecks.

The notion that employers should be willing to pay for experience is valid up to a point—the point where experience no longer counts in a fast-changing job or industry. Sometimes experience works against people by trapping them in old ways of thinking and doing.

A key skill that may or may not come from experience is judgment. Good judgment comes from your thought process. And an entrepreneurial thought process fosters sound decisions.

## Run That by Me Again

Interacting for the past 18 years with other business owners (as a member of five professional associations) and continually overdosing on articles and books by and for entrepreneurs, I've repeatedly observed these traits about entrepreneurs: They're intense. They're confident. They're doers rather than talkers. They plan, they do, they keep score. They're always in a hurry. They're good time managers. They're careful not to offend others with insensitive remarks. They're excellent conversationalists. They ask a lot of questions. They listen well. They seek challenge. They show passion. They learn from failures. They like to win.

## Rate Yourself

How many suggestions do you typically submit to your organization each year? _____

What's the dollar value of these suggestions? _____

Do you make decisions about your daily tasks and projects as if you owned the business?

_____ Yes _____ No

Do you consider your boss your client?

_____ Yes _____ No

Do you take personal responsibility for all your team does or fails to do?

_____ Yes _____ No

# You Mean We Have to Pay for All That?

Budget Appropriately

### The Skill, Trait, or Attitude

A budget is a comprehensive quantitative plan for using money during a specific time period. As the person responsible for the budget, you have an overview of the work and projects that need to be completed, allocate appropriate amounts to accomplish each project, and then stay within those spending boundaries as you accomplish the goal.

### Uses on the Job

Budgeting for sales and marketing of your product or service

Budgeting inventories and production in your department

Budgeting cost of goods sold in your own small business

Budgeting administrative expense in a fund-raising project for your community

Budgeting capital expenditures for items in your department or affecting your team responsibilities

Budgeting cash for bonus incentives at the end of the year

Budgeting to accomplish a specific project

### So Why Should I Care?

Miracles happen with unlimited cash. The real challenge is in making miracles happen within budget parameters. As anybody knows who has prepared a budget for a few years, the tendency in preparing one is to be overly optimistic about projected revenues and to understate expenses. But as John Ray's nursery rhyme goes, "If wishes were horses, beggars might ride."

A safer mind-set when budgeting is to project both revenues and expenses as "best case" and "worst case." Compare your best and worst conditions and prepare a reasonable forecast and budget with figures somewhere in between. Then continually review and adjust your numbers.

Budgeting controls the future health and growth of a department or company. Many growing companies have grown themselves right out of business because of a lackadaisical attitude about budgeting. Money in, money out, the faster it came in, the faster and looser they saw it go out. No matter how well things are going, eventually someone has to manage that growth with a budget.

Whoever controls the budget controls the future. The only issue remaining is the time frame for that future. A wildly successful, growing company can be brought to the brink of bankruptcy by a person holding the purse strings who operates without benefit of a budget.

## Rate Yourself

Do you establish and maintain a family budget?

_____ Yes    _____ No

Do you measure and record growth in your personal net worth from year to year?

_____ Yes    _____ No

Have you established your own personal financial goals and saving and spending plans for the next year? Five years? Ten years?

_____ One year    _____ Five years    _____ Ten years    _____ No

Do you know what your actual versus projected expenditures and revenues were last quarter?

_____ Yes    _____ No

Consider smaller budgeting projects on the job or for a civic project as a learning exercise. Make projections on revenue or production. Set budgets. Measure your projections against your actual performance. Record the principles learned for future budgeting situations.

# So Are We Making Money Yet?

## Understand Common Business Terms and Profitability Ratios

### The Skill, Trait, or Attitude

You understand the *why* of what businesses do and understand the actions businesses take because of that why. You can make quality decisions about financing options, staffing, scheduling, marketing, purchasing, and pricing and explain those decisions based on solid business reasons.

### Uses on the Job

Purchasing parts from suppliers, determining whether to spend the dollars up front versus waiting until orders are taken.

Determining whether and when to hire additional staff

Determining whether a specific marketing campaign generates profitable leads

Setting or raising prices for new products or services

Buying the latest technology

Determining an appropriate price reduction to increase market share

Justifying your profit margins when customers demand discounts

Writing a business plan to secure a loan

### So Why Should I Care?

Just how important is it that employees become business literate? The purchasing, hiring, scheduling, marketing, or production decisions they make as employees; the

**85**

records they keep; the explanations they give when questioned by customers, stockholders, or investors all may come back to haunt the employer.

Here are some of the major decisions and happenings that rest on the explanations employees provide and the actions they take:

- Investors/stockholders monitor management's performance.
- Prospective investors decide which companies to invest in.
- Banks and other lenders decide whether to make new loans or continue existing loans.
- Stockbrokers and money managers and analysts make buying recommendations to their clients.
- Suppliers plan their production accordingly.
- Customers make purchase decisions based on the financial soundness of your company.
- Managers review their past performance and plan the future.
- Competitors plan their strategies based on your performance, direction, and mistakes.
- Governmental representatives decide how to investigate, tax, and regulate your company.
- Politicians and various advocate groups decide whether to investigate, support, promote, or fight your company or its products.

Since decisions and information have been pushed down to empowered employees, everyone in the company needs to understand how his or her job affects the big profit picture.

## Rate Yourself

Briefly define these terms:

capital _____

working capital _____

equity _____

term loans _____

subordinated debt _____

line of credit _____

receivables turnover _____

inventory turnover _____

gross margin _____

net profit _____

return on investment _____

liquidity _____

quick ratio _____

current ratio _____

return on assets _____

market share _____

Do you know the profit margin on your primary product or service?

_____ Yes    _____ No

Do you know last year's growth rate in revenues for your company?

_____ Yes    _____ No

# So Who's in Charge Here?

Lead Productive Meetings

## The Skill, Trait, or Attitude

You can lead a meeting, assuming all related leader responsibilities: selecting an appropriate site, inviting the appropriate attendees, developing a clearly focused agenda, facilitating discussion, managing group dynamics to minimize the effects of problem situations or problem participants, making assignments, and planning follow-up actions.

## Uses on the Job

Leading a meeting to inform others about events, facts, actions, policies, products, or services

Leading a meeting to gather information or opinions

Leading a meeting to brainstorm solutions to problems or options for a project and to evaluate those options and make a decision

Leading a meeting to gain buy-in from others

Leading a meeting to persuade or motivate others to take action or change an attitude

## So Show Me...

The 3-M Company has been tagged as the "meeting expert." The company estimates that its managers spend a total of 4.4 million hours annually in meetings. Consider your own time and that of others in your department spent in meetings, and do a little figuring to calculate the meeting cost in salary alone.

So what can go wrong to sidetrack meetings and waste these hours and dollars? A study of meetings by the

Annenberg School of Communications at the University of Southern California found six factors commonly linked to meeting disasters: lack of notification, no agenda, wrong attendees, lack of control, politics, and hidden agendas. All of these potential problems fall within the control of the leader.

Let me define success and failure with two examples:

First, the meeting failure: A training instructor called a sudden meeting immediately as the class day ended to "evaluate and get reaction" from attendees about a new training program. There was no agenda. Instructional design experts were not in the room. Five other instructors who might be asked to lead the class were present. Only three "real" attendees (who would use the training to do their job) were present.

The meeting leader began the meeting with an opening statement that she was dissatisfied with the pilot class and considered it too difficult for the average learner. She called on the five other instructors present to offer an opinion. The five instructors insisted that they didn't really have an opinion about the design but did think they would have to do more preparation to teach it than they typically do. The three "real" attendees gave it rave reviews.

The meeting leader held the floor herself for 85 percent of the discussion time, and then summarized the meeting with this statement, "So we've concluded that the new training program isn't suitable for our company and that we should just stay with the training program we're currently using." One last note: The meeting leader was the designer of the program that the company was currently using and that had been labeled by the senior executives as ineffective.

Result: This company continued with an ineffective training program that their own employees began to boycott as a waste of time.

Second, the meeting success: Another company had an outside vendor develop a four-day proposal-writing course and present a pilot program to 25 sales managers responsible for the field sales force. The meeting leader announced that an evaluation meeting would be held on the day following the class to determine the appropriateness of the course. At the end of each day, the meeting leader distributed an evaluation "think" sheet for attendee reflections on that day and an agenda for the Friday evaluation meeting.

On the Friday meeting day, the leader announced that because she had a vested interest in the outcome of the course evaluations, she would like to withhold her opinions until the end of the meeting. She brought in an outside facilitator to lead the two-hour evaluation process. The outside facilitator led the group of 25 managers through an intense evaluation of each course module and its use for their sales force and their varied tasks.

At the conclusion of the meeting, the 25 sales managers gave the course an objective numerical rating that led to a clear decision about the course. They thanked the meeting leader for developing a course that so clearly met the needs of their sales force.

Result: The meeting leader of this company won accolades. The meeting attendees felt good about giving input about their needs. The company adopted this excellent training program for worldwide use. They began winning more business because their salespeople wrote more effective sales proposals.

As a meeting leader, you may wield great power over decisions and outcomes—more than you should if you share misguided notions about the leader role. For example, if you don't facilitate discussion so that all sides get heard about an issue, you become ultimately responsible for mediocre decisions. If you don't lead the group through an effective brainstorming and evaluation process for decisions, you contribute to poor, costly decisions.

## Rate Yourself

Evaluate the last five meetings you've led:

|  | Yes | No |
|---|---|---|
| **1.** Did the meeting start and end on time? | ☐ | ☐ |
| **2.** Did you prepare a clear, focused agenda? | ☐ | ☐ |
| **3.** Did participants come prepared with appropriate information? | ☐ | ☐ |
| **4.** Did all participants contribute to the meeting? | ☐ | ☐ |
| **5.** Did you refuse to let the group sink into "group think"? | ☐ | ☐ |
| **6.** Did you accomplish your meeting objective? | ☐ | ☐ |
| **7.** Did others not invited sabotage your plans? | ☐ | ☐ |

How often do others select you to facilitate discussion?

_____ Often          _____ Sometimes          _____ Rarely

# We've Got to Stop Meeting Like This!

Participate Actively in Meetings

### The Skill, Trait, or Attitude

As a productive meeting participant, you contribute ideas, opinions, and expertise confidently. You remain alert to the meeting processes and order of discussion. You can express disagreement without being disagreeable and hostile. You respect others' time by avoiding repetitive comments and digressions and answers to questions no one is asking. You arrive on time, prepared with the appropriate information, and avoid unnecessary interruptions and absences.

### Uses on the Job

Brainstorming with several members of a client organization about how best to solve problems for them

Contributing ideas on a project for your own organization

Suggesting sales goals during the annual sales meeting

Evaluating as a committee how a supplier has performed for several departments in your organization

Working on a proposal development team

Participating in a team interview session to hire new staff

### So Show Me...

As a productive participant you can sometimes measure your own output and effectiveness simply by contrasting your typical meeting behavior with the irritating, nonproductive behaviors of coworkers. Here's a sampling of meeting participants who give their coworkers migraines:

- The nonparticipants: These attendees are present physically, but not mentally. They refuse to speak up with necessary information, never generate or interject new ideas, and ride the fence on decisions.

- The windbags: These people feel compelled to comment on *every* idea and insist on answering questions no one is asking.

- The interrupters: These participants show no awareness of discussion stages or decision-making processes. The group may have evaluated all the pros and cons of four options, have decided on Option C, and have made assignments for implementation when the interrupter circles back to discuss the pros of an alternative option.

- The pessimists: These people feel compelled to always present the downside of things. Their comments dissuade, discourage, and demotivate.

- The attention getters: These participants spout off-the-cuff, zany opinions just to get a rise out of others and keep the spotlight on themselves.

- The gurus: These attendees state opinions as if they were facts and refuse to acknowledge their own faulty assumptions or invalid conclusions. They intimidate others who may express concerns or opinions that are contrary to their own.

- The time bombs: These participants explode emotionally at inappropriate times.

- The yes-man/yes-woman types: These participants withhold their true opinions, concerns, or information rather than risking confrontation or conflict. They publicly agree but may privately complain or sabotage.

## Rate Yourself

Consider the last five meetings you've attended as you respond to the following questions:

Did you arrive on time, avoid interruptions, and stay until the meeting ended?

_____ Yes _____ No

Did you come prepared with appropriate information?

_____ Yes _____ No

How many relevant opinions or ideas did you contribute to the discussion? _____

Did you express any disagreement confidently, but without aggressiveness?

_____ Yes _____ No

Did you maintain your emotional composure?

_____ Yes _____ No

Did you feel heard and understood?

_____ Yes _____ No

Did you leave with increased awareness, information, or commitment to the group decision? Why not?

_____ Yes _____ No

Because _____

Did you leave with a clear understanding of follow-up actions to be taken?

_____ Yes _____ No

# I Just Didn't Like the Guy

Influence and Persuade Others to Gain Consensus

## The Skill, Trait, or Attitude

You influence others to open their minds to your ideas, opinions, information, or recommendations. You interpret facts or data in light of others' interests and help them understand how they can benefit from supporting your recommendations or decisions. You build credibility for your ideas either through your own track record for success or by thoroughness of preparation with supporting data. You are adept at uncovering reasons for resistance and effectively address those areas of concern to bring people to a decision. You depend on both a logical and an emotional appeal to persuade.

## Uses on the Job

Selling your product or service to customers and prospects

Persuading suppliers to provide excellent customer service and offer discounted pricing

Motivating coworkers to contribute their best efforts on a project

Persuading a potential employer to hire you

Persuading an investor or banker to lend you money

Persuading activist groups to support your cause

Soliciting volunteers or money to complete a community project

Influencing another company to form a partnership with yours to offer a more complete product or service

Getting buy-in from your fellow team members to follow your suggested course of action

## Explanation

According to Aristotle, our efforts at persuasion depend on three characteristics. To get other people to do what we want them to do, we need to 1) reason with them logically, 2) understand what motivates them and create an emotional response, and 3) display integrity and trustworthiness so they believe us.

First, logic. You need to make a strong case for what you're trying to persuade them to do. You do the homework required, no matter how tedious. You take the surveys, you gather the data, you measure the production, you find comparable businesses who've had success with what you're advocating. You state what you know for a fact and point out your assumptions that seem to make sense.

Next, emotions. You appeal to others' basic instincts for self-worth, physical needs, protection, and belonging: What is immediately important to them personally? What do they want to have (money, prestige, fun, opportunity), be (successful, happy, healthy, loved) , feel (comfortable, important, free, admired), or avoid (criticism, stupidity, worry, wasted effort)? To reach people emotionally, you have to appeal to these desires and feelings.

Finally, your track record for truth. Why should others trust you? Your credibility grows in direct proportion to how often you've been right, accurate, and truthful. Your credibility is diminished by mistakes and intentional ambiguities.

Influence and power are not synonymous. Being influential is the result of selling one's self, the validation of personal passion. The ability to influence grants power *without* coercion.

## Rate Yourself

How often can you persuade an airline or hotel agent to accommodate an unusual request?

\_\_\_\_\_ Often     \_\_\_\_\_ Sometimes     \_\_\_\_\_ Rarely

Do family members tend to take your advice on personal decisions?

_____ Often  _____ Sometimes  _____ Rarely

Have you ever been asked to give a motivational speech— for example, an appeal for charitable contributions for a civic cause or a request for volunteers on a project?

_____ Often  _____ Sometimes  _____ Rarely

Are coworkers generally satisfied that you know what you're talking about when you make recommendations, or do they probe for more information and often seek other opinions before making a commitment?

_____ Often  _____ Sometimes  _____ Rarely

Does your presence tend to have a calming effect on others caught in a crisis? Do they tend to put you in charge in emergency situations?

_____ Often  _____ Sometimes  _____ Rarely

Do others seek you out to help them get someone to change something he or she is presently doing?

_____ Often  _____ Sometimes  _____ Rarely

# So How Much Would You Take for Your Car?

Negotiate Win-Win Outcomes

## The Skill, Trait, or Attitude

You can work out amicable, profitable agreements between people who have different goals and different ideas about how to arrive at those goals. You confer with others to understand their viewpoints and needs and to explain your own so that together you can settle a matter with both of you feeling good about the resulting arrangement.

## Uses on the Job

Determining who gets which office when you move into a new workspace

Negotiating with a supplier or customer about pricing, quality standards, and delivery arrangements

Agreeing with a supervisor or staff member about a raise, transfer, or promotion

Negotiating with someone in the graphics department to change the production schedule and deadline for your urgent project

Negotiating the details of a lease or purchase

Agreeing on the response time for support service you need for your office equipment

Working with an angry customer to resolve a problem about service that the customer considers inadequate

## So Show Me...

Once you establish the relationship, the environment, and the pattern for negotiations, the spirit of agreement prevails. One of my most successful relationships began with negotiations with Encyclopaedia Britannica's corporate training group, now a new entity called The Training Edge.

The Britannica executives attended one of my sessions at a convention in the early 1980s. After the program, one of their representatives came up to the platform and asked me outright, "Would you be interested in letting Britannica purchase video rights to your new book and produce a video of your writing program?"

I rolled the question over in my mind (for about half a second) and said, "Possibly. Yes, very possibly!" She said, "Good. How about breakfast tomorrow morning with our two vice presidents and CEO?"

We began discussions that next morning about what *I wanted* from a producer. That was a novel approach, I thought, coming from a company whose name was a household word. I gave them my list of wants. Then they stated their list of wants. We struck a deal and began the first project.

But the negotiations had just begun. Here were the kind of give-and-take discussions that followed the real discussion: They wanted a link to all the publicity I was getting from the media about my first published book. So I suggested that I take a booth at the trade shows they attended, adjacent to the Britannica booth—that way I could explain the video design and concepts to their booth visitors and ours. And, of course, it would be logical for them to pay for my booth exhibit and travel fees for all my staff, wouldn't it? They agreed. So, my newly organized and low- to no-budget company began its first marketing effort.

Then we got into the marketing of the product. What if I decided I wanted to use the video vignettes with some of my larger clients? No problem, they said. That doesn't hurt our sales. We'll edit the custom videos for you for free. I owed them one. Then they wanted to introduce the video product with a big splash. Would I attend an autograph party at the Boston Hyatt Regency for 500 of their key clients—without charging them my day consulting fee? Sure, if they would let me display my other noncompeting products to the same clients. They did; I did. Another win-win.

Then we encountered our first difficulty. Was I going to get a commission on the leads I turned over to them—while standing in *my* trade show exhibit booths that *they* paid for? It didn't seem reasonable even to me, so they got those leads. Then when their rep called on a client of mine—but in a new region of the country—did I get the commission on that sale? Their response? If you say it's your client, it's your client. No questions asked.

Well, to make a long story and relationship shorter: We struck three more video–book deals. They gave me their blessing to go to the competition to produce another video that they couldn't get their own people to sign off on as a good potential project.

Two months ago, I got a mailer from them saying they'd partnered with the U.S. Chamber of Commerce for new distance learning options via satellite delivery around the world. I phoned to tell them about my newest book to be released in the fall. They pitched it to the powers that be in Washington, and now we're in the newest technology loop for corporate training, thanks to that long-term relationship. Another win-win.

According to poet Ralph Waldo Emerson: "Nothing astonishes men so much as common sense and plain dealing."

## Rate Yourself

When you anticipate making a major purchase such as a car or house, do you enjoy or dread the discussion of details and pricing?

_____ Enjoy    _____ Dread

Before you enter negotiations, do you research the situation and establish your must-have's, nice-to-have's, safeguards, and time frames before you begin to work out an agreement?

_____ Yes    _____ No

Do you close negotiations feeling as though you've compromised your original goals? Or are you typically pleased with the outcome of your negotiations?

_____ Compromised    _____ Pleased

If forced to choose one classification or the other, would you typically consider those involved in negotiations with you as comrades or adversaries?

_____ Comrades    _____ Adversaries

Is the other party typically pleased with the outcome of negotiations with you?

_____ Yes    _____ No

How would you rate yourself regarding your ability to negotiate successfully?

| Seldom | Sometimes | Usually |
|---|---|---|
| ____ successful | ____ successful | ____ successful |

# I'm Caught in Their Crossfire

## Mediate Conflicts of Others

### The Skill, Trait, or Attitude

You can intervene to resolve disagreements and mend relationships (between others) so that the conflict doesn't escalate to affect the working environment and productivity of an entire group. You can stay focused on the objectives of both parties and not become emotionally hooked. You can help both parties reach their goals and meet their needs without becoming the enemy of either.

### Uses on the Job

Mediating between two buyers in a customer's company (for example, the technical guru and the department manager) who both want to buy from you but who disagree about how to structure their own differing needs into the deal

Mediating between administrative support people who disagree on how to handle registration for the upcoming seminar you're hosting

Mediating between two people vying for the same promotion to work for or with you

Mediating between two senior executives who have different, conflicting ways to assess your department's performance

Mediating between two team members who disagree on how best to tackle an assigned team project

Mediating between two long-term employees to decide who drives the new truck

# *Tips*

- Intervene only when asked. For the most part, people don't like to have others poke their noses into what they consider their own business. The only trouble with that laissez-faire attitude is that it can hinder the productivity of all concerned.

- Avoid "taking sides" and talking the opposition over to the other viewpoint. Make it clear from the very beginning that you want to be objective and work with both people. Although you may talk with them separately, make sure they know that you will be passing along what they each tell you so that you can identify, verify, and clarify differences and agreements along the way. If you don't warn them, they will invariably think you're breaking their confidences, and they will lose trust in you as an impartial mediator.

- Pass along the criticism and compliments each gives about the other. Sharing the positive remarks adds credence to the negative comments. Your goal is to help each person see the merit in the other's viewpoint. To see the merit, they have to face the facts and opinions honestly, without questioning the other's intentions.

- Point out where you think they have both miscommunicated in the past—wrong information, invalid assumptions, misjudged intentions, and inappropriate or incorrect conclusions. Then remind them of common goals again and again. Summarize their own needs and goals and ask them to suggest resolutions. Be careful about imposing your own solutions to their problems. If you do that, both may feel that you have your own agenda and have ignored theirs.

- Help them keep the lines of communication open. Look for opportunities to invite them to interact on various projects from time to time. Gradually, you can back out of your role as referee. Reinforce their positive actions that contribute to open communication.

## Rate Yourself

Recall a specific situation in your work arena in which you observed conflict between two people. Try to recall your mind-set during the matter as you respond to the following questions:

Did you engage in discussion with only one person about the difficulty and not with the other?

_____ One       _____ Both

Did you avoid being sucked into the conflict?

_____ Sucked in       _____ Remained objective

When confronted by both warring sides, did you offer your own solutions or lead the people involved to suggest their own solutions?

_____ Mine       _____ Theirs

Do you currently have a good working relationship with both people involved?

_____ Yes       _____ No

Do the two individuals or groups have a good working relationship now?

_____ Yes       _____ No

# Over My Dead Body

Resolve Conflicts of Your Own

## The Skill, Trait, or Attitude

You can settle problems involving conflict over facts, goals, circumstances, personalities, and values. With a conflict of information, you can ask the right questions to gather appropriate facts, reexamine assumptions, and draw valid conclusions to correct errors. With a conflict of goals, you can create alternatives so that both you and the other person have your needs met. With a conflict of circumstances, you can reason together to generate new limits, new details, or new choices to change a situation.

With personality conflicts, you can control your behavior and emotions so that they do not hinder your productivity and keep you from working with another individual. Because conflicting values can rarely be resolved, you recognize such a conflict and take appropriate action: You either tolerate the different viewpoint or decide to align yourself with others with values similar to yours.

Caught in a conflict, you make a conscious choice about whether to accommodate, compromise, overpower, or collaborate with the other person. You act, rather than react, in a negative situation.

## Uses on the Job

Resolving conflict over expectations about the service a supplier provides

Resolving a personality conflict with a team member who has a negative disposition about most ideas offered in team meetings and demeans people

Resolving conflict about how often to perform maintenance procedures on equipment

**105**

Resolving conflict with a supervisor about the priority of your tasks and responsibilities

Resolving conflict about how you gather information on a competitor and how you use that information

Resolving conflict about how frequently you must travel out of town to meetings that involve your project team

## So Show Me...

I'd be willing to wager that Thomas Paine also referred to home building when he said, "These are the times that try men's souls." Having built three houses myself in the last few years, I'd have to conclude that the entire process has built-in opportunities for delay and dispute.

With the last builder, we had conflicts that fit just about all the categories above: a conflict of facts, a conflict of circumstances, a conflict of personalities, and a conflict of goals.

First, the conflict of facts. I said the building contract called for shelves around all four walls in our kitchen pantry; the builder said it did not. (The fact: Our spec sheet to the builder of "wants" did contain the shelving, but the builder had not transferred that list to the specs appended to the contract.)

Second, the conflict of circumstances: The trim man had not included the shelving in his original estimate and someone—either we or the builder—was going to have to pay for them.

Third, a conflict of personalities: The builder was a disorganized person to whom details and paperwork were bothersome; on the other hand, I like to have things in writing.

Finally, the conflict of goals: I wanted the shelves; the builder wanted his set profit margin.

How did we resolve it? We verified the *facts* about the contract. We agreed on the *circumstance* that the trim man had to be paid extra by someone. The organized versus disorganized *personality* quirks could be contained for the limited six-month period of construction. The only thing that remained was the *goal*. Very tactfully, the builder proposed the predicament this way: "The entire shelving will cost only $900 extra. I don't want you to be unhappy with me over a minor $900 issue. We want a good referral from you. Although I don't think I should have to, I'll put in the shelves at my expense." Result: I told him to put in the shelving and that I'd pay for it.

He reexamined his big-picture goal and decided that a glowing reference was of utmost importance. I reexamined my goal of keeping the builder happy so that he would come back to repair and service the inevitable little things that crop up after move-in and decided that paying $900 extra for the shelving would accomplish the bigger goal.

Conflicts, large and small, are resolved through flexibility and accommodation.

## So Why Should I Care?

A director of human resources related this conflict to me: "I need help with four executives who are supposed to be a team but can't work together. We have a multi-billion-dollar project that needs to get done, and our CEO hand-picked these four people because of their specific background and expertise. They each head up one of our subsidiaries. Two of the men don't like each other and don't respect each other's expertise.

The third man has simply withdrawn from the whole mess and refuses to talk to either of the first two. And the fourth is a lone ranger who wants to do the entire project himself and considers conferring with the other three a waste of time. I can't even get them to attend a meeting to discuss things. The CEO says for me to do whatever it takes—bring in whoever it takes at whatever cost—to get these guys off dead center. The entire future of the company is at stake."

Although most conflict situations revolve around lesser issues, conflict resolution can be the difference between profitability and failure, between a job and a job hunt, between a winning proposal and a losing bid.

No matter what your level of expertise, unresolved conflict can bring all progress to a standstill.

## Rate Yourself

- Have you ever pulled together a business deal when there was an initial conflict over facts, circumstances, personalities, or goals?      Yes   No
- Do you deal with anger constructively?      Yes   No
- Do you handle difficult personalities effectively?      Yes   No
- Do you feel comfortable confronting others about problems?      Yes   No
- Do others seem comfortable confronting you about a conflict?      Yes   No
- Are most of your relationships with coworkers short-term or long-term?      Short   Long
- Are most of your personal friendships short-term or long-term?      Short   Long

# Yeah, Yeah, I'll Give It Some Thought

Solicit Usable Advice
and Feedback

## The Skill, Trait, or Attitude

You are comfortable asking others for advice or feedback. You know how to ask the right questions and relay the appropriate details to solicit pertinent advice and feedback. When you receive advice and feedback, you analyze it relative to your own criteria and goals for decisions and actions.

## Uses on the Job

Seeking advice about a selling strategy with a specific customer prospect

Soliciting feedback from a supervisor about career options

Asking a coworker for suggestions to handle a difficult staff member working with you on another project

Polling colleagues in the industry about whether attending a particular trade show would be beneficial

Soliciting recommendations for an appropriate speaker for an upcoming association event

Asking industry professionals about appropriate marketing strategies for your new service

Seeking opinions about people who might be appropriate to serve on your advisory board for a new entrepreneurial adventure

Asking fellow professionals whether a certain position would further your career goals

## Explanation

If we're not careful, the advice or feedback we receive can be largely our own. Many times we telegraph the answer or opinion we want to the other person, as with these kinds of statements: "I just completed eight dazzling graphics for this proposal. Don't you think I'll do better with Vendor A if I walk in with a full-blown proposal rather than a brief letter?" Or: "I've asked for a transfer to Chicago to work with our MIS division. Do you think I'll have a shot there to handle the larger projects?" If the listener has a heart at all, she will reaffirm your action or decision—or at the least withhold any doubts and opinions altogether.

Wording plays a big part in soliciting objective feedback and a clear analysis of a situation. For example, do you want *ideas, insights, information, affirmation,* or *personal experience* from the other person? Be clear about exactly what you want to know.

Equally important is asking for advice or feedback based on criteria you can clearly articulate. When we're traveling, my husband is in the habit of asking anyone within earshot for recommendations of sightseeing opportunities: "Can you recommend some good restaurants around here?" or, "What good local tours have you taken?" As a result of such general inquiries, we've evaluated our meals in many places, making a game of trying to decide what the criteria were for referral: low price, nearby location, pay-as-you-go service, a brother-in-law who's the manager? Since my husband seldom specifies likes or dislikes, we get some odd answers. On the occasions when he's a little more specific in his request ("Can you tell me where we can get a great seafood buffet nearby without having to dress up?"), we typically are better pleased about where we eventually end up for dinner.

The flipside of not being specific in your request for advice is giving the other person so much information that he becomes as overloaded and puzzled as you are. Selecting pertinent details means using an objective filter as you pour them into another person's head.

Finally, receiving usable advice or feedback sometimes involves accepting input from multiple sources. As each contributor offers comments, you can analyze the feedback with regard to that specific source's credibility, philosophy, and values.

## Rate Yourself

When you walk out of your doctor's office, are you clear about the options he or she has outlined for your good health? (If not, did you ask probing questions to clarify?)

_____ Clear _____ Unclear

How often do you pay for, but not take, your legal counselor's advice? (If you consider the advice poor, are you sure you outlined the situation with all the pertinent facts and your goals?)

_____ Take advice _____ Ignore

If you toss out a situation for decision to a group of friends, do they tend to agree or disagree in their advice? (If they all tend to agree, your presentation of the situation was probably slanted in one direction.)

____ Objective ____ Slanted
presentation presentation

When you receive career advice from a colleague or supervisor, do you routinely consider the success of the person giving it?

_____ Consider _____ Ignore

# You Go First!

Admit Mistakes or Errors
in Judgment

## The Skill, Trait, or Attitude

You own responsibility for your work. You do not have difficulty in accepting the consequences of decisions you make and admitting errors. You do not give excuses for mistakes on routine matters, justify a judgment error, blame others for inaction, or cite circumstances for lack of initiative.

## Uses on the Job

Admitting miscalculations in a report

Admitting lack of results or follow up-on assigned projects

Admitting a hiring mistake—a mismatch between person and job

Admitting forgetfulness about attendance at an important meeting

Admitting failure to follow specifications on a customer's order

Admitting violations of company policies and approved procedures

Motivating your coworkers or staff by referring to your track record with words or actions

## So Why Should I Care?

Frequently the most disappointing element in discovering a mistake is in bringing that mistake to the attention of the persons responsible: Often their reactions reflect character flaws.

A case in point: Scheduled to speak before a corporate audience, I arrived at the resort the day before the meeting just to mix and mingle with the group and check out the staging and equipment. After an hour or so on-site, I discovered that the client had not duplicated my packet of materials for the audience members. Somehow the client liaison on-site had no information about what had happened; all she knew was that she didn't have the packet originals.

Immediately, I phoned my office and discovered that Barry in our shipping department had tried to send the packets but had had difficulty in locating the right person. The client had referred him from one person and address to another. When he hadn't received a return phone call from his second phone message, Barry simply selected one of the two addresses and mailed the packets anyway. Having heard nothing to the contrary from the client, he assumed all was well.

When I returned to the office after the speaking engagement, I discussed with Barry, a new employee, his lack of follow-up and my expectations for the future. Here was his hostile response: "So I get blamed when the U.S. Post Office doesn't do its job?" I pointed out that he wasn't getting blamed because the U.S. Post Office didn't perform, or even because the package wasn't at the right location. He was being asked to be thorough about follow-up on future packages to make sure they arrive and that the client does, indeed, have them in hand before an event.

Did he understand the difference then? He continued to tell me that he made two phone calls without receiving a return call, that he noted in the file that he had *tried,* that the client liaison should have noticed the packets were missing, and finally that the audience members didn't need the packets anyway.

Did he *ever* understand the difference? A few months later, when Barry was terminated, another supervisor made the same observation: "Barry just can't or won't understand what he's responsible to do. When I try to tell him about mistakes, he just shrugs them off."

The only difference between an entry-level employee and an executive is the seriousness of their mistakes; unwillingness to admit and correct errors is an identical flaw in character at any level.

## Rate Yourself

How often do you acknowledge an error or weakness to a client, customer, or coworker?

____ Seldom      ____ When appropriate      ____ Often

How often do you acknowledge a mistake to your supervisor?

____ Seldom      ____ When appropriate      ____ Often

How often do you acknowledge a mistake to a family member or friend?

____ Seldom      ____ When appropriate      ____ Often

# So Who Are You to Tell Me?

Be Receptive to Negative Feedback and Positive Suggestions

## The Skill, Trait, or Attitude

You are willing to listen to negative feedback with an open mind. Even if you cannot totally agree with someone's comments about a situation or your performance, you look for some validity in the comments so that you can learn from them. You actively solicit feedback with the intention of using it to improve your performance and results.

## Uses on the Job

Soliciting feedback from a prospect about why your proposal was not selected

Soliciting feedback from an interviewer about why a candidate other than you was chosen for promotion

Soliciting feedback from a long-term customer about why another vendor was awarded the contract your company wanted

Surveying employees about their opinions on your management style

Asking team members to play devil's advocate with your ideas and recommendations voiced during project meetings

## So Why Should I Care?

Here's a conversation I overheard at lunch between a project manager at a large software firm and her sister-in-law.

I'm trying to decide who to send to Australia for a big installation coming up in a few weeks. I'd send Benny—I'm sort of mentoring him—but I've got some reservations.

Like what?

His language. He can really talk pretty rough. I've grown used to putting up with it in the office. But I don't know whether he could control it on a customer's site for as long as an installation takes.

So why don't you talk to him about it?

I tried once—when he first got moved into my department. On a performance appraisal, I stepped out of my role as manager and told him that I was just talking as a friend but that I thought his foul mouth might hold him back. And he very quickly pointed out that my own boss used the same kind of language. And he's right.

So you're not going to send him to Australia?

I guess not. It's one thing to talk like that around here. That's internal, we're used to it. But I can't afford to upset a client—he'll be around too many people there. I'm just not sure that he understands it's a matter of professional etiquette.

So the high-potential Benny did not receive the plum assignment because his boss and friend had tested the waters of negative feedback and found them shallow.

Consider how many times you yourself have thought about giving some helpful, but negative, comment to a friend or coworker but have refrained because you didn't know how receptive the person would be. Has the situation ever been reversed?

## Rate Yourself

Place a checkmark beside the behaviors you've noticed in yourself when you anticipated or received negative feedback:

Becoming defensive with an emotional reaction _____

Trying to shift the discussion to another topic _____

Responding with "Yes, but ..."     \_\_\_\_\_

Preparing your rebuttal rather than listening to the details     \_\_\_\_\_

Counterattacking by finding flaws in the other person or what the other person has done or plans to do     \_\_\_\_\_

Displaying body language that says, "I'm bored and this discussion is ridiculous"     \_\_\_\_\_

Being too busy to talk     \_\_\_\_\_

# I've Already Told You Once

Give and Follow Clear Instructions

## The Skill, Trait, or Attitude

You give clear instructions and follow instructions from others. You can present an overview to others and understand the big-picture goal (the overall intention) and the measurable outcome necessary on specific projects. You chunk the information into doable steps or processes. You state or verify the deadline. You state or verify the available budget—upper and lower limits—and other resources to complete the project. You warn of or verify any potential difficulties that may occur during the task and create confusion. You show willingness to clarify or make adjustments as necessary.

## Uses on the Job

Telling or verifying how to prepare a report

Telling or verifying how to install new computer hardware

Telling or verifying how to complete an engineering project

Telling or verifying how to investigate an accident

## Rate Yourself

Circle the number below that best describes you as an instruction follower:

1. Give it to me step by step—and not so fast.
2. I've got it, I've got it already—and if I don't, I'll figure it out without your help.
3. You should already know that I don't do well with this sort of stuff.

4. That step reminds me—what course do you play when you go to Florida? ...

5. Just write it down; I'll get to it later.

6. Let's go through it once, and then I'll try it alone. And I'll need a quick reference and a phone number in case I have questions or problems down the line.

Circle the number below that best describes you as an instruction giver:

1. Here's a manual (a book, an article, a phone number, a fax number).

2. Just hold on. I didn't tell you to do that yet. Don't get ahead of me.

3. Let me give you a little history first. Then we'll look at the project a little later on.

4. It's easy. Just watch me. Nothing to it.

5. You know how to do that, don't you? (asked with a scowl). You don't need instructions, do you?

6. Let's get you productive—first a brief overview of what this is all about and then you can get your feet wet while I'm here to troubleshoot.

# Well, You Said to Use My Own Judgment, Didn't You?

Delegate So Things Get Done Right

## The Skill, Trait, or Attitude

You trust other people to carry out projects and tasks in your area of responsibility. You select the right person for the job by evaluating his or her experience, training, and personality. You give an overview of the project or situation so that the delegatee has a full grasp of what's involved, including resources, time frames, and budget. You set up effective feedback and control methods to ensure that the person ends up on target. You use delegation to develop your staff, increase their job satisfaction, and improve their morale.

## Uses on the Job

Delegating routine tasks that you don't have time for so you can devote more time to higher priority or more complex matters

Delegating projects for which a subordinate has better knowledge or more expertise than you

Delegating projects as training for staff members to stretch their capabilities or to assess their profitability

Delegating projects during emergencies or your absences from the job

## Run That by Me Again

Given the pleasant opportunity to delegate away their jobs while still collecting a paycheck, why don't more people delegate more often? Both real and perceived reasons hold people back:

Some people fear losing control of projects and tasks for which they are ultimately responsible. Giving someone full rein on a project may mean giving them freedom to fail. And who wants a failure on their record? If the delegator has had a bad experience in delegating a previous project, and has had to suffer the consequences when a subordinate dropped the ball, he or she may be fearful of a repeat performance.

Others refuse to delegate because they want their own thumbprint on every project. They want to have input and make all the key decisions.

And some people with big egos think no one can possibly do a job as well as they themselves can. If they do by chance delegate a project to someone who does the job well, they feel threatened by the delegatee's success.

Some people hesitate to share information. To do a job well, the delegatee needs numbers, facts, and records that may previously have been privileged information. Delegators may resist letting go of that information.

So to alleviate all the above fears and hesitations as a delegator, you have to select the right person for the right job, set up the standards of quality that you expect in the end product, and establish firm checkbacks to give you comfort about retaining control.

Having learned to delegate effectively, few people will ever want to stop the process.

## Rate Yourself

How often do delegated tasks get done to your standards, on time, and within budget?

_____ Most of    _____ Not often    _____ Rarely
       the time        enough

When you delegate, which of the following do you always include?

_____ Overall goal or mission

_____ Tangible output/end product

_____ Budget and other resources

_____ Time frames/deadlines

_____ Standards for measuring success or failure

How do the delegatees feel at the conclusion of a project?

| _____ Proud of their achievement | _____ Puzzled and/or frustrated | _____ Angry because of failure |
|---|---|---|

# I Just Did What You Told Me ...

Appraise the Performance
of Others

## The Skill, Trait, or Attitude

You can evaluate the performance of others—either colleagues, staff, or vendors—and determine whether they are meeting the objectives you or your organization have set for them. You demonstrate an understanding of the goals and objectives. You can identify ways to measure results. And you can give accurate feedback and assessment of performance.

## Uses on the Job

Judging whether to renew a long-standing vendor contract

Investigating previous work and references given by a potential bidder to determine whether to award a contract for new work

Conducting an objective performance appraisal

Recommending one of your staff members for a promotion, transfer, or task assignment

Awarding incentives and recognition to staff members for their achievements

Determining the amount and timing of a merit pay increase

## So Show Me...

It's not enough to know good performance when you see it; you also have to recognize poor performance when you see it. That is often the more difficult of the two skills.

I learned the hard way when I hired my first salesperson several years ago. He worked for our organization for 14 months without making a single sale. So why didn't I do a better job of guiding him, or why didn't I terminate his employment much sooner? I failed in all three areas of the task just defined above.

First, I didn't have a clear objective for what he should achieve in what time frame. Because I had no industry averages for what he should be able to sell, I took a "let's wait and see what's possible" approach. He came to our organization from a Fortune 500 company and touted his awards for ranking in the top 10 percent of their sales staff. So, I reasoned, he should know how to sell, shouldn't he?

Second, not only did I not set a clear goal or objective for total sales revenue at the end of the year, I failed to devise *any* way to measure success—not number of leads, not appointments made, not proposals or quotes submitted.

My third mistake was in the area of feedback about his performance. When we had conversations about leads, opportunities, and efforts, I asked questions about each situation. But I simply listened to his explanations and excuses without communicating my reservations about how he was handling the various prospects. I just assumed that he was equally aware and concerned about his own lack of progress. In lieu of straightforward feedback, I tried to offer encouragement and gave him options and preferences about how to handle his territory.

When I was finally at wit's end about his lack of results, I decided to give him a test on product knowledge and learned that he could not even articulate all the benefits of our products and services, much less their appropriateness for certain customers.

Failure on all fronts. Robert Louis Stevenson summarized our situation succinctly: "The cruelest lies are often told in silence."

## Rate Yourself

Would your staff or coworkers say you have given them clear goals for their tasks?

_____ Yes _____ No

Do you have clear, consistent standards for measuring progress and results of others' work? Do the people being evaluated understand the standards? If you handed them a blank piece of paper and allowed them five minutes, could they list the criteria by which they'll be measured at the end of the next performance period? Would they say you applied those standards evenly at the end of each period and with every employee doing a similar job?

____ Yes to all ____ Yes to some ____ No to all

How often do you withhold straightforward feedback about performance because you like someone personally?

_____ Withhold feedback _____ Provide feedback

Have you ever withheld approval (a contract, a raise, a promotion, a project) from someone because you didn't like him or her personally?

_____ Yes _____ No

Have you ever assigned someone you didn't like to a task you knew could not be accomplished, thereby ensuring failure?

_____ Yes _____ No

# So Where Did You Say the Goal Line Was?

Coach Others to Success

### The Skill, Trait, or Attitude

You can train, instruct, support, and motivate others to improve their performance. Specifically, you understand the overall goal of the organization, and you can identify ways an individual can become more effective in that environment. Through questioning techniques and informational dialogue, you can help others to see where their performance can be improved. In short, you can lead others to decide what to do, why to do it, and how to do it.

### Uses on the Job

Coaching a new employee to improve his or her contribution to a team project

Coaching a less senior employee to be eligible for promotions

Coaching one of your own staff members to be able to take over your job so that you can move up or on in the organization

Coaching a peer through his or her preparations for a presentation during the annual corporate meeting

Coaching a friend or family member in an entrepreneurial endeavor in which you have special expertise or experience

### Run That by Me Again

In their book, *The Coach,* Steven J. Stowell and Matt M. Starcevich, Ph.D., associated with the Center for Management and Organization Effectiveness, provide an excellent explanation of the differences between coaching and a performance appraisal. I've translated their ideas to the following chart:

| Coaching | Appraisal: |
|---|---|
| **When/How** | |
| Interpersonal influence in response to need or opportunity | Formal feedback offered at set times to determine how someone measures up to external standards/objectives |
| **Who** | |
| An individual who wants to take advantage of help | All employees who report to a specific manager |
| **Why** | |
| A spontaneous reaction to improve performance or attitude for the purpose of learning and for future career choices | A determined action to document strengths and weaknesses, to compare performance with predetermined standards, to document the employees' value to the organization, and to support management decisions |

## So Why Should I Care?

Coaching completes the sports metaphor that has so often been useful in describing behaviors and options in the work arena. Companies have flattened their organizations and ridded themselves of middle managers and their accompanying appraisal forms. As a result, we have done away with the often dreaded straightforward evaluation, but have sorely missed the helpful information from supportive supervisors.

Coaching has brought back the instruction and feedback, minus the judgments and recordkeeping. Star athletes seek the best coaches. Star corporate performers seek the best coaches.

## Rate Yourself

Could you tell or show someone else how to succeed in your job?

_____ Yes _____ No

Can you lead an employee to reach *his or her own* career objectives rather than your objectives for that individual?

_____ Yes _____ No

Can you lead an individual to improve performance in a problem situation when he or she doesn't seem motivated to change?

_____ Yes _____ No

# I Tried to Tell 'Em, but They Wouldn't Listen

Become a Leader

## The Skill, Trait, or Attitude

As a leader, you inspire followers—those who follow voluntarily, not as a result of coercion or position. Your leadership involves a set of skills, an attitude, and a character that influences other people.

## Uses on the Job

As a team leader, leading your group to develop a new product or service

As a consultant, leading a client to respond to change and improve the profitability of the organization

As a manager, leading a customer service department to improve customer satisfaction through better service on the same products

As a director, leading a department to improve its performance based on higher standards and resulting in more experienced employees

As a coworker, leading two new employees to make suggestions to improve a process or a system

As a manager, leading your department through a successful merger with another company

## Run That by Me Again

Leaders focus with great intensity on a task or goal. Leaders stay the course—they are determined. Leaders bounce back from setbacks and overcome obstacles. Leaders are energetic. Leaders are dependable. Leaders practice what they preach. Leaders have integrity—they keep their promises and honor their commitments. Leaders generate trust.

Leaders define reality. Leaders create a vision. Leaders take calculated risks. Leaders understand the broader picture. Leaders ask the right questions. Leaders use resources effectively. Leaders feel responsible for the future as well as the present. Leaders look for learning.

Leaders care about their followers. Leaders feel responsible for establishing positive morale among their followers. Leaders help followers reach their potential. Leaders exhibit competence. Leaders serve humbly. Leaders communicate honestly—they share information, articulate ideas well, and express their own vulnerabilities with candor.

## Importance on the Job

"Where there is no vision, the people perish," according to Proverbs 29:18. Leaders provide the vision and mark the path that others in the corporation follow.

## Rate Yourself

According to Max Depree, CEO of Herman Miller and author of *Leadership Is an Art,* the evidence of leadership is in the followship:

| | | |
|---|---|---|
| Do you have followers? | Yes | No |
| Are your followers reaching their own potential? | Yes | No |
| Are your followers serving the customers, their coworkers, and the shareholders? Are they achieving the desired results? | Yes | No |
| Are your followers willing to accept change and manage conflict if you say so and lead the way? | Yes | No |

Are you leaving behind a value system that
others can embrace?                                    Yes    No

Are you building both a structure and lasting
relationships?                                          Yes    No

# So What Do You Expect Me to Do about It?

Be Resourceful

## The Skill, Trait, or Attitude

You handle situations and solve problems in ways not immediately apparent to the typical person. You think quickly and creatively on your feet and discover how to use whatever space, equipment, information, or staff at hand to keep a situation under control.

## Uses on the Job

Offering a reasonable explanation to a potential buyer when the prospect's primary contact is unavailable

Taking charge at the scene of an accident to minimize damage and ensure the safety of other people

Completing duplication and assembly of 1,000 manuals to be shipped despite the fact that the on-site copier equipment breaks down

Finding a way to add graphics to a proposal without having access to the usual graphics software program

Ensuring that all employees hear the CEO's speech firsthand even though there isn't a large enough assembly room on-site

Completing a project on time and within budget despite being understaffed

## Run That by Me Again

Children today are typically less self-reliant and resourceful than children of a decade ago. It's not uncommon for ten-year-olds to expect their parents to keep them entertained—with toys from Fisher Price, with video movies from Blockbuster, with playmates chauffeured to their front door, with sports organized by the city. When parents feel pulled in so many directions, they frequently get the urge to turn on a child and demand, "Go entertain yourself for awhile."

The same happens in the workplace between employers and employees or between buyers and sellers. The real challenge is getting the work done *without* all the information at your fingertips, *without* the latest equipment on the market, *without* the best facilities, or *without* the optimum staff. Being resourceful involves looking at the goal or problem with new eyes and finding an alternative way to reach it or solve it. Being resourceful means turning "It can't be done" into "How can it be done?"

## Rate Yourself

When faced with a problem or major project, do you expect someone to provide you with all the optimum resources to accomplish the task?

_____ Yes    _____ No

How successful were you with the last project that demanded alternative or makeshift technology, staff, or facilities?

_____ Unsuccessful    _____ Successful
_____ Very successful

Do you seek out challenging or routine tasks?

_____ Challenging    _____ Routine

Are you frightened, awed, or excited about challenging assignments?

_____ Frightened    _____ Awed    _____ Excited

# I Once Had an Idea ...

Practice Creativity

## The Skill, Trait, or Attitude

You habitually think about things "out of the box." You frequently ask *why* and *what if* to make changes for the better—or sometimes just for the sake of change. You trust your instincts and act on intuition. You can take others' ideas and apply them in new ways—to create new processes, new systems, new products, new services, or new solutions.

## Uses on the Job

Inventing a new product or designing a new service to offer customers

Creating a new document layout to make information more accessible to the skimming reader

Creating a new computer language

Developing a new customer service policy that calms irate customers who enter your place of business with a problem

Finding a new solution to an old problem

Discovering a way to reduce production costs

Perfecting a unique question or test to use in interviewing job applicants or independent contractors to determine their potential job performance

## Run That by Me Again

German physiologist and physicist Hermann von Helmholtz, writing in the late 1800s, first identified the four steps of the creative process: preparation, incubation, illumination, and verification.

The preparation stage includes your education and your experience. Particularly, this phase involves your saturating yourself with information about the problem to be solved or the dream to be realized.

The incubation step involves assigning the problem or goal to your subconscious mind to percolate. During this stage, your prior experience, thoughts, and information intermingle on a subconscious level during your conscious downtime. In other words, you forget about the issue and go about other things.

The third stage, illumination, just happens. A creative idea or solution to a problem simply pops into your mind from nowhere. Eighteen years ago as a writer, I developed the habit of keeping pen and paper at my bedside. Then in the car. Then by the bathtub. Then in the pocket of my exercise sweats. The best ideas came at inopportune times—a new plot twist for my novel, persuasive wording to use in a client proposal, or a great analogy for a motivational speech. I was initially puzzled about why I always got the best ideas when I was "not working," but I've since learned more about this stage of the overall creative process. Convenient, no, but profitable, yes.

Finally, the last stage in birthing a creative idea is called verification. This is the exciting part—trying out the idea to make sure it works. During this stage, you may refine, revise, tweak, piggyback, trim, or expand the original idea.

## Tips

To put yourself in the path of creativity, put yourself in the right frame of mind:

- Prepare yourself by saturating your mind with applicable information and viewpoints.
- Allow yourself downtime in which you can simply daydream and play.
- Learn to be comfortable with ambiguity and seemingly contradictory thoughts, alternatives, and facts.

- Unhook your mind's evaluation mechanism—particularly, remember that it's unreliable and dangerous to evaluate new ideas too soon.
- Break things down in their simplest forms to think about them.
- Question everything.
- Risk being wrong.

## Examples

In the sports arena, creative thinkers have melted down old tennis shoes to make a basketball gym floor, one much easier on the feet and ankles of players.

In medicine, creative thinkers have taken discarded placentas of a newborn baby and injected it into children suffering from leukemia in lieu of a bone-marrow transplant.

In finance, creative thinkers have paid cash rebates to people who charge purchases on their credit cards.

In music, creative thinkers have composed songs with computers rather than strings.

In television, creative thinkers have put news around the globe on the hour, every hour.

In transportation, creative thinkers began to price air travel as cheaply as the bus or train.

In retail, creative thinkers began to make bookstores reading rooms and chat corners.

## Rate Yourself

How do you respond to "weird" ideas that come to you?

_____ Censor them      _____ Try them out

Do you consciously assign things to your subconscious mind for processing?

_____ Yes      _____ No

Are you willing to be wrong in front of other people about a hunch?

_____ Yes      _____ No

# But I Never Forget a Face

Exercise and Develop
Your Memory

## The Skill, Trait, or Attitude

You can remember figures, facts, faces, and names. You can recall the details of your experiences—what you did, why you did it, and how you did it. You remember the histories of clients and customers and of projects, policies, and procedures. You can read or hear information, tuck it away in your mind, and recall it when you need to use the information.

## Uses on the Job

Calling a prospect by name when he or she walks up to your trade-show booth unexpectedly

Relocating a statistic that you read in a published industry survey to use in a proposal

Giving references (contact name, company, title) immediately when asked by a prospect during a sales call

Recalling an anecdote from your experience to use in illustrating a key point while giving a presentation

Repairing a piece of equipment as a result of recalling the same symptoms in an earlier equipment breakdown

Listening to a technical presentation and then applying the information from the presentation to your work weeks later

## So Why Should I Care?

If you're thinking that computer technology has replaced human memory, think again. Although computers have been a boon to efficiency and provided a permanent memory for our current explosion of information, they have two major drawbacks: We don't always have them with us, and when confronted with new, unprogrammed problems and issues, they haven't yet simulated human reasoning.

## Rate Yourself

Can you remember your address and phone number from two residences ago?

_____ Yes    _____ No

How many names of former professors can you recall?

_____

Can you remember the central idea of the last three programs or symposiums that you attended that were sponsored by your professional organization?

_____ Yes    _____ No

Do you remember all the major terms of the last contract you negotiated? Would you stake the outcome of the next contract on that recall?

_____ Yes    _____ No

Do you recall the amount of your typical electrical bills? Would you recognize it if the current bill was unusually high?

_____ Yes    _____ No

After a power outage, can you reset or reprogram your VCR, clocks, phones, and household appliances without looking at the instruction manuals?

_____ Yes    _____ No

Can you remember how to perform annual maintenance on a major piece of equipment in your office?

_____ Yes    _____ No

Can you look at your key client list and recall exactly what percentage of your total business those companies represent?

_____ Yes  _____ No

Do you remember within a few hundred miles when it is time for your 3,000-mile oil change?

_____ Yes  _____ No

Do you remember within a few weeks when the consultant's contract is to be renewed?

_____ Yes  _____ No

# So What If I Don't Want To?

## Motivate Others

### The Skill, Trait, or Attitude

You provide others with a reason to act and excel. You share a vision and excite them about meeting a goal. You inspire them to work for the common good, not just their self-interests. Based on your understanding of human nature in general and personalities in particular, you design both intrinsic and external rewards to cause others to care deeply about the job they're doing.

### Uses on the Job

Motivating people to complete a complex project that drains them physically, mentally, and emotionally

Motivating a poor performer to improve his or her work to acceptable standards

Motivating long-term employees to accept difficult changes in processes, policies, or personnel

Speaking to a group of community citizens to motivate them to adopt policies and attitudes favorable to your organization

Soliciting contributions—both money and volunteer time— for a charitable cause sponsored by your organization

Asking your employees' cooperation in reducing expenses to improve profits

Instilling shareholder confidence in your efforts to turn around a declining business

Inspiring confidence among prospective customers that you can do the job they want to their satisfaction

## Run That by Me Again

Motivation can't be left to convention keynoters. Although we tend to tag someone in a formal leadership role at the top of the organization with the label "motivational," motivation needs to happen throughout the ranks. Even peers on a team can ignite the motivational spark that inspires their group to produce excellent work.

So what does it take to be motivational? For the most part, motivation stems from attitudes and actions: Motivators communicate consistently high standards. Motivators praise others generously. Motivators keep others informed. Motivators care about others—their physical well-being and their peace of mind. Motivators see other people as important within themselves, not simply as a means to an end. Motivators use tact in their communication about deficiencies and weaknesses. Motivators show confidence in others' abilities. Motivators are realistic about what others can produce. Motivators work as hard or harder than the people they lead. A key word in the motivator's vocabulary is *we*.

Demotivators, on the other hand, set unrealistic goals. Demotivators belittle people for making mistakes. Demotivators take all the glory for group achievements. Demotivators "say it like it is"—from their own viewpoint—without a thought for tact or appropriate phrasing. Demotivators remain rigid in their opinions and decisions. Demotivators discourage creative thinking and resourcefulness. Demotivators tell people what to think and how to think about it. Demotivators play favorites and pass out penalties or rewards based on varying standards and preferences. Demotivators give little thought to their employees as people but rather view them as tools to get a job done. Demotivators consider themselves above the rules and policies set for others. Demotivators assign others the unpleasant, difficult tasks while keeping the plum projects and benefits for themselves. A key word in the demotivator's vocabulary is *I*.

## Rate Yourself

Would your coworkers ever voluntarily select you as their team leader?

_____ Yes    _____ No

Has someone ever *voluntarily* canceled scheduled time off to work with you in completing a project?

_____ Yes    _____ No

Are your subordinates stretching themselves to learn, grow, and take on new responsibilities or perform the routine ones more effectively?

_____ Yes    _____ No

Have you ever been amazed or even moved to tears by the commitment your coworkers or subordinates have shown in reaching a goal or accepting a challenge you've set for them?

_____ Yes    _____ No

# Here's What I Plan to Do—Anybody Have a Problem with That?

Interact Productively with Others on a Team

## The Skill, Trait, or Attitude

You work cooperatively with others and contribute to the team effort with information, ideas, opinions, emotional support, time, and shared tasks. As a team member, you set mutual goals, plan, listen to others, resolve conflict, build consensus, present ideas assertively, recognize others for their contributions, and articulate your team efforts to outsiders.

## Uses on the Job

Working as a team to improve product quality

Working as a team to increase productivity on an assembly line

Working as a team to improve a process

Working as a team to improve employee skills

Working as a team to improve customer service to clients

Working as a team to develop employee participation in setting policies

Working as a team to a solve an assigned problem

Working as a team to recruit, interview, and select a new employee, independent contractor, or supplier

## So Why Should I Care?

Zenger Miller, an international consulting and educational firm, in conjunction with the 10,000-member Association for Quality and Participation, recently reported findings from a survey of U.S. and Canadian companies about their involvement in teamwork. Here are two of their key findings:

First, the majority of team members believe they are very successful in achieving their objectives of improved quality, greater customer satisfaction, improved productivity, and employee skill development. Team members, however, point out that their success is highly dependent on support from top management.

Second, teams struggle with a host of problems, including the most prevalent ones of inefficient meetings, inadequate resources, and performance problems among their individual team members.

Conclusions we can draw from these survey findings? Effective teams have big payoff potential. Ineffective teams often fail because individual members lack skills or exhibit defeating behaviors and attitudes regarding teamwork.

## Rate Yourself

| | | |
|---|---|---|
| Do you withdraw and pout when things do not go your way in a team meeting? | Yes | No |
| Are you impatient with team members who can't see things your way or follow your work style? | Yes | No |
| Do you reject insights from other team members and often feel competitive toward them? | Yes | No |
| Do you try to go around or even sabotage others' decisions when you think they are poor ones? | Yes | No |

Do you do less than your best on individual
assignments from the team and frequently          Yes   No
miss team deadlines?

Do you complain to others outside the team
about the internal workings of your team or        Yes   No
about other team members?

As a team leader, do you take the opportunity
to push through your own agenda and your
own biases about how things should be done         Yes   No
rather than gathering input and building
consensus?

Do you prefer individual awards and
recognition to team awards and recognition?        Yes   No

# So Who Says I Have To?

Be Cooperative

## The Skill, Trait, or Attitude

Cooperation is the opposite of competition. With a cooperative mind-set, you respect others' talents, needs, and goals. You can empathize with others' feelings and limitations and can see things from their viewpoint. You have a tendency to look out for the well-being of others, as well as your own. You focus on the higher duty or bigger goals, above your own. As a result, you give synergistic effort to achieving group goals.

## Uses on the Job

Contributing information and effort to the sales team preparing a proposal

Restructuring a department or division and deciding to recommend some of your key people for the new slots

Giving up a key account as a salesperson because top management is experimenting with a new way to divide sales boundaries

Providing excellent customer service so that satisfied customers return to buy again

Relaying unrequested but helpful information to someone in another department

Volunteering to work on a team to design a new employee policy that you personally will not benefit from

Allowing your administrative assistant to transition into a new position in another division by working afternoons in the new division for one week before actually beginning the new job

What causes an uncooperative attitude? Stubbornness. Pride. Laziness. Jealousy. It's sometimes stronger to give an example of what something is not:

Flying from West Palm Beach, Florida to Minneapolis, I had a one-hour stopover in Atlanta. We sat on the runway for 57 minutes of that hour. But as we finally jolted to a full stop and saw the red light blink off, indicating that it was safe for us to leave our seats, I still had hopes of dashing for my departing plane. The flight attendant had announced the gate directly in front of ours as the departure gate for the next leg of my flight.

Sitting in the second row of coach, I had only one passenger in front of me. And when he rose rather slowly, acting as if he had all the time in the world, I started to ease past him with, "Excuse me, please, Sir. I have three minutes to make my next flight."

To my surprise, he didn't budge. Instead, he planted his feet in the center of the aisle and glared down at me with a scowl. "If I missed my flight, you're going to miss yours. Just hold on." Then he slowly pulled his bags from the overhead rack, leisurely searched them for a sweater to pull over his head, and then deliberately blocked the aisle as he sauntered off the plane.

Do similar situations happen during the typical workday—among employees working in the same company for the same ultimate goals? Of course they do.

I recently received a call from the education coordinator at a client's office, who was trying to ready things for our next seminar. Could we immediately ship her 24 books for the attendees? Someone from the purchasing department, she assured us, would get in touch in a few days to give us the billing information. We sent the books.

A few weeks later, we phoned the responsible person in the purchasing department to ask about the paperwork. She had no paperwork, knew nothing about the order, and did not have time to check on it for us. We waited.

Two days later, a second person in the purchasing department phoned to order 24 books. We explained that the 24 books had already been sent. He insisted that he didn't know anything about the first 24 books but that his paperwork said for him to order 24 books. We mentioned the high probability that this was the same order we had already shipped. Could he please check that out? No, that wasn't "his department." We gave in and accepted the second order, shipping another 24 books and billing with the purchase order number he gave.

Three days later, the person called back to say he had too many books. He accepted no blame, saying that the person who told us to ship the books in the first place "was out of line." Would we accept the returned books? Yes, we would.

An hour later, we got a call from the education coordinator in another branch about another seminar. Would we send 20 books? We explained that the purchasing department had just called, asking permission to return 24 books, and we suggested that they shuffle those books down the hall, rather than going to the trouble, expense, and delay of returning them to us. Sure, she said, no problem.

The next day we got a call from the purchasing department, asking why we were billing for two shipments of 24 books. We gave the caller all the details, including the names and phone numbers of her colleagues, and asked her to work out the problem. No, she insisted, the education coordinators had no business phoning us themselves. No, she would not contact them to straighten out the mess. "Let them take care of it themselves."

I phoned the education coordinator to verify that I should indeed send the extra books and not depend on the switch. How dare the purchasing department, she grumbled, mess things up! Would she take the other names and phone numbers from me so she could straighten out the problem? No, she said. It was the purchasing department's fault; let them contact her.

The next day ... well, I won't bore you with the rest of the logjam. You can probably think of several similar incidents of your own.

What causes an uncooperative attitude? Stubbornness. Pride. Laziness. Jealousies—comparing your paycheck or workload or abilities to someone else's. Perhaps resentment, a sense of someone's not pulling his or her own weight, and a feeling of frustration at having to "pick up the slack."

Some people approach all their work projects with this same attitude: We're all in this separately. That attitude creates crevices in a landscape increasingly scattered with teams.

## Rate Yourself

Are you stingy with information?

_____ Stingy       _____ Open

Do you frequently envision yourself competing rather than cooperating with other people in your own department or division?

_____ Competitive       _____ Cooperative

How often do you put yourself out to help someone when you cannot see an immediate, tangible benefit for yourself or your own work group?

_____ Rarely       _____ Often

Would you rather work on a project alone or with others?

_____ Alone       _____ With others

# I'd Like to Thank Tom, Dick, and Harriet

Give Others Credit for Their Help

## The Skill, Trait, or Attitude

You acknowledge others' ideas and efforts on successful projects and either give them recognition yourself or see that the appropriate people notice and reward them. You do not feel that others' successes diminish your own.

## Uses on the Job

As a team member, giving credit to other team members who help you complete a project successfully

As a consultant, giving credit to customers who help resolve their own problems and make you look good as a vendor

As a buyer, recognizing the value your suppliers contribute to your success

As a salesperson, giving credit to the support staff who help service customers and keep them happy

As a supervisor, giving credit to employees who help you meet department goals

## Run That by Me Again

Writer William Dean Howells observed, "I know, indeed, of nothing more subtly satisfying and cheering than a knowledge of the real good will and appreciation of others. Such happiness does not come with money, nor does it flow from a fine physical state. It cannot be bought. But it is the keenest joy, after all; and the toiler's truest and best reward."

What would keep a person from giving credit where it's due? Selfishness. Egotism. Insecurity. Dishonesty. Ignorance about what made a project successful. None of these traits or attitudes paints a pretty picture.

Credit and praise cost nothing and pay big dividends to others and yourself.

## Rate Yourself

List five coworkers or customers you've praised or given credit to in the last month:

1. _____
2. _____
3. _____
4. _____
5. _____

How often do you acknowledge someone else's excellent work in front of others?

_____ Seldom     _____ Often

How often do you write a note of appreciation to the author of a book or article that gave you new insights or inspired you?

_____ Seldom     _____ Often

How often do you stand in line after a presentation to thank a speaker for an informative or inspiring talk?

_____ Seldom     _____ Often

How often do you write letters to recognize the professional and capable service you received from a hotel clerk, car rental agent, or flight attendant?

_____ Seldom     _____ Often

# What Do You Mean, You Don't Agree with Me?

## Understand the Value of Diversity

### The Skill, Trait, or Attitude

You acknowledge the benefits that people with diverse characteristics and experiences bring to the workplace. Beyond age, race, gender, or mental and physical abilities, you recognize a plethora of influences on people that affect their values, opportunities, perceptions, and work: education, family status, military experience, work experience, religion, language, geographic residence and travel, economic status, relationships, and skills.

Your behavior toward others who are different is not condescending, belittling, or arrogant. Instead, you offer compassion, respect, and opportunity.

### Uses on the Job

Selecting team members to work with you on a project

Selecting individuals to serve on a team to develop policy for all employees in the organization

Developing strategy to appeal to a specific customer or prospect

Identifying appropriate awards and recognition for star performers across the nation or around the world

Resolving conflict among employees who must work closely together

### So Why Should I Care?

A workplace that acknowledges the value in diversity focuses on establishing an environment and culture that welcomes and rewards each person for his or her achievements. Years before the current diversity emphasis burst on the scene and into our consciousness, Ralph Waldo Emerson observed, "You must pay for conformity."

Uniformity can strangle profits. In a global economy, businesses that understand and cater to only one culture will find their market for products and services very limited. A diverse employee group provides the best competitive advantage to innovate with new products and services demanded by a diverse world market.

## Rate Yourself

When given the opportunity to select colleagues to work with you on teams or committees, do you tend to select other people who think like you and share similar backgrounds?

_____ Similar   _____ Different

List five people you admire. How many are of another gender, race, or age group?

| Name | Gender | Race | Age Group |
|------|--------|------|-----------|
| 1. _____ | _____ | _____ | _____ |
| 2. _____ | _____ | _____ | _____ |
| 3. _____ | _____ | _____ | _____ |
| 4. _____ | _____ | _____ | _____ |
| 5. _____ | _____ | _____ | _____ |

With whom do you spend your spare time, downtime, or personal time? Considering the many characteristics mentioned above, are these friends more similar to or different from you?

_____ Similar   _____ Different

If you had to set policy for a large number of people, to what extent would you seek out the opinion of people with different characteristics (as listed above)?

____ Wouldn't think about it   ____ Would seek diversity

# Aw, Shucks, It Weren't Nothing

Be Humble about Your Skills and Achievements

## The Skill, Trait, or Attitude

You have an accurate evaluation of your own skills. You understand your strengths and your weaknesses and can articulate them to others without undue pride or arrogance. You do not use your skills and achievements selfishly to wield authority over others.

## Uses on the Job

Encouraging people to offer suggestions for better ways to do things

Interviewing people for their honest input on a sensitive issue

Building credibility and support for a message or cause (rather than commanding compliance)

Inviting wide participation from team members who may have an inclination to let the more qualified carry the load

Allowing others to receive recognition without interjecting your contribution to the effort or project

## Run That by Me Again

Don't confuse self-deprecating humor and comments with humility. Humility does not mean undervaluing and denying the things you do well. Humility involves an accurate, not inflated, sense of self-importance.

Pride, on the other hand, causes you to look down on other people, particularly those who are less skilled or intelligent. Pride also leads to self-deceit and blindness about personal shortcomings. Full of pride, you tend to gloss over any weaknesses pointed out to you. You typically blame others when things don't turn out well.

When you have a distorted sense of self, other people feel repelled rather than attracted to you. Despite your achievements, skills, and expertise, others tend to shun you rather than seek you out for conversation and companionship.

When you have an accurate, not inflated, sense of self, other people are attracted to you because of your competence and achievements. Others seek you out and enjoy your company. They'll frequently comment to you (or to others about you) that despite your great success, you seem so approachable and personable.

## Rate Yourself

Take your pulse on pride:

| | | |
|---|---|---|
| Do you enjoy controlling access to people or information? | Yes | No |
| Do you enjoy giving other people orders? | Yes | No |
| Do you enjoy approving or rejecting others' plans? | Yes | No |
| Do you keep a mental checklist of how your job skills rate in comparison to others? | Yes | No |
| Do you consider your job title, bank account, automobile, or home to be a good measure of your success as a person? | Yes | No |
| Do you ever have the urge to tell someone else how much you earn or how much your business is worth? | Yes | No |
| Do you enjoy throwing your weight around as a buyer because you hold a responsible position in a large organization? | Yes | No |

# Give It to Me One More Time

Analyze and Learn from Failure; Be
Teachable, Approachable, Coachable

## The Skill, Trait, or Attitude

You recognize failure as part of the professional growth
process; it does not destroy your confidence. You do not
blame others for failures that are your own. You analyze
why you failed on any given project and identify why and
how to do things differently in the future. You welcome
feedback offered by others and look for principles and information for future improvements.

## Uses on the Job

Being willing to ask a long-term customer why you lost the
new contract

Asking a prospect why he or she did not buy from you

Deciding what you will do next time to keep from missing
a project deadline, overspending the budget, or falling
short of the expected results

Talking with a coworker who seems distant to learn what
destroyed the comfortable relationship you had

Analyzing what you did that was demotivating, rather
than motivating, to the people whom you had wanted to
take action

Rethinking your actions that caused you to lose a job or
promotion

## Run That by Me Again

You may fail for any number of reasons: incompetent
coworkers, ambiguous goals, unexpected circumstances,

inadequate resources, job demands that are beyond your experience or expertise, lack of forethought or planning, inadequate information.

Whatever the cause, failure can result in growth. We learn lessons:

- That we can't please all the people all the time
- That risk taking is, well, risky
- That we have skill deficiencies and weaknesses
- That we can cope with disappointment and difficulties
- That we don't control the world
- That our goals are sometimes inappropriate
- That new goals or situations are more worthy of our attention

Failures become permanent only when we fail to learn from them.

## Rate Yourself

Write five important principles or skills that you have learned primarily as a result of failures rather than successes:

1. _____
2. _____
3. _____
4. _____
5. _____

# Did I Miss Anything?

Be Punctual; Meet Deadlines

## The Skill, Trait, or Attitude

You have a good sense of timing. You respect time—yours and that of other people. You are punctual for your workday and prompt for meetings. You set project deadlines for others with care, and you meet the deadlines others set for you.

## Uses on the Job

Being punctual for client appointments or team meetings

Being available for scheduled conference calls

Turning in both routine and special reports on time

Completing steps in a project by interim dates and projects by final due dates

Interviewing for a job

## So Why Should I Care?

When you are a new employee, contractor, or supplier, your "buyer" doesn't have much history upon which to judge your work. Therefore, issues of attitude take on grave importance. Punctuality represents an entire range of attitudes about a job, a boss, or a customer.

The CEO of a large international office supply and furniture company told me about his fire drill routines at 8:05 a.m. in the parking lot. The story his employees tell (and he confirms) goes like this: When the $200 million company experiences a downturn, management weeds out their weakest performers. At 8:05, they assemble everyone in the parking lot. Those who are present in the parking lot keep their jobs; those who arrive later are sent home with a pink slip. To this particular CEO, the lack of punctuality represents a poor attitude and disrespect for the job.

The same happens routinely in job interviews. A candidate who cannot make it to a job interview on time will pose a risk every time he or she must meet with a client.

Some may argue that in this day and age of flextime and varied lifestyles punctuality becomes less important. Granted, most companies do allow flexible work schedules, but no matter what time the employee elects to begin work, others expect him or her to be available at that time.

Technology has made people more, not less, impatient. We count time in nanoseconds. Yes, we have portable computers, modems, satellite hookups, Internet links, and e-mail so that we do not have to interact with each other in real time. We can send and receive messages when it's most convenient to us individually.

But when we set a *real-time* meeting, phone call, or presentation, we expect people to synchronize their clocks and psyches and be available. The cost of keeping even ten people waiting five minutes to begin a meeting can be calculated in the thousands of dollars.

## Rate Yourself

For my routine workday, I am:

_____ Always     _____ Punctual     _____ I never
       punctual          most of              notice—
                         the time             who cares?

For meetings, I am:

_____ Always     _____ Usually     _____ Often
       punctual          punctual           late

For scheduled phone calls, I am:

_____ Always     _____ Available most     _____ Often
       available         of the time              late

Regarding project and team deadlines others set for me, I:

_____ Usually     _____ Am often     _____ Rarely
meet them           late                 pay
attention
to them

Regarding project and team deadlines I set for myself, I:

_____ Usually     _____ Am often     _____ Disregard
meet them           late                 them if
they're
incon-
venient

# Once You Stop the Bleeding, It's Not All That Painful

Be Positive and Pleasant; Show Enthusiasm and Drive

### The Skill, Trait, or Attitude

You habitually demonstrate a positive outlook on life in general and your work in particular. Your body language, behavior, and actions reflect a pleasant, upbeat attitude as you interact with coworkers and customers. You expect the best of others, until they prove that opinion about them is unwarranted. You accept assignments with a can-do attitude. When you disagree with issues, policies, procedures, projects, or reasons, you disagree without being disagreeable. You are solution-focused, not problem-focused.

### Uses on the Job

Leading a team to complete a difficult project

Generating referrals to grow your business

Motivating others to do their best on assignments

Motivating yourself to complete difficult or unpleasant tasks

Maintaining your morale when forced to work around negative people

### Run That by Me Again

According to TV journalist and broadcaster Hugh Downs, "A happy person is not a person in a certain set of circumstances, but rather a person with a certain set of attitudes." I couldn't agree more.

**161**

Pessimism reflects a way of looking at the world. The pessimist has gained that worldview through a lifetime habit of interpreting events in a negative way: 1) Pessimists see the bad as a permanent, rather than a temporary, condition. 2) Pessimists see bad as the general condition of the world, rather than an aspect limited to occasional isolated, specific situations. 3) Pessimists see themselves as targets for the bad, rather than seeing negative events as random and external. Their motto could be summed up this way: "Things are bad and they won't get any better. Why do things like this always happen to me?"

Optimists, on the other hand, show enthusiasm about their jobs and have a habitually positive way of looking at the world: 1) Occasionally, bad things happen to good people. 2) This negative thing shall come to pass, and then life will be good again. 3) Okay, so I got knocked right on the head on this one—tomorrow will be better. Their motto could be summed up this way: "Some days I'm the windshield; some days I'm the bug. Most days, I travel fine."

## So Why Should I Care?

Companies cannot afford to chance sabotage by keeping a negative person on the payroll. What fears do these unhappy people create?

- They quit on the job. They simply stop putting out the effort to do a good job.
- They spend their time looking for the next job, which they think will be a little better (but never is).
- They spread gloom and doom to other people and drench the whole workplace in a downpour of negativity.
- They refuse to offer suggestions for improving systems, processes, products, or services. Why should they contribute to a company that has done them wrong?
- They frequently take things (equipment, secrets, supplies) to make up for the bad they see themselves as having to put up with.

Positive people, on the other hand, spread their enthusiasm. They build morale. They give every job their best shot. They look for ways to make things better, contributing ideas for continuous improvement. After all, if the company benefits, they assume things will get better for them personally, too.

That is not to say that positive people always agree and welcome every project with open arms. It does mean that they can disagree about or dislike a *specific* project, policy, or procedure and still maintain an enthusiastic, upbeat attitude about their work and their company.

Given a choice between a highly competent, negative person who affects other people's morale for the worse and a very positive person of average competence, the odds will favor the positive person every time for long-term contribution. Why? As one CEO put it, "You can teach skills; you can't teach attitude."

## Rate Yourself

When given a new assignment, which is closer to your typical reaction?

**A.** Here we go again—another stupid (useless, wasteful, wrong, difficult, unfair, boring, impossible) project.

**B.** Here we go again—another intriguing (necessary, worthwhile, right, easy, reasonable, fun, doable) project.

# We've Got a Problem

Solve Problems

## The Skill, Trait, or Attitude

Problems keep people or organizations from reaching their goals. As a problem solver, you recognize a problem when you see it, determine its causes, brainstorm possible solutions and their effects, identify the best alternative, and take action.

## Uses on the Job

Arranging to get a credit line when you foresee cash flow problems

Determining how to alleviate the overcrowded conditions in the warehouse

Improving the sagging productivity of the staff

Changing the organization's image with the public

Recruiting more highly qualified engineers

Improving workflow through a division of the company

Raising customer satisfaction about the service you provide

Handling a larger volume of calls with the same number of operators

## So Why Should I Care?

The workplace is full of Goliaths, chanting "Take me on." What we need are more Davids armed with a slingshot and courage.

## Tips

- Determine if the problem is solvable. As defined, some problems are unsolvable. Butting your head against a wall can be costly and time-consuming.

164

- Make sure you're solving the real problem. Keep asking *why* until you trace the problem to its real cause.
- Try to state the problem positively rather than negatively. (Not "How can we reduce customer complaints?" but "How can we increase customer ratings of our service?") It's always easier to work toward a positive goal rather than a negative one.
- Write things down. Holding all the pertinent facts in your head makes for foggy thinking. Forgetting even one key detail can skew your thinking. Laying the problem out in black and white can improve your analysis.
- Don't hold out for the perfect solution. Once you start with some improvement, you or others can often piggyback ideas. Try for the "best under the circumstances" until the circumstances or goals change.
- Pay attention to your gut as well as your intellect. What's logical isn't always sensible or right. Hunches and experience lead to quality solutions as often as forced, logical structure does.

## Rate Yourself

Outline your procedure for solving this problem:

Company XYZ recruits new employees with no set preference for either male or female salespeople. Their hiring records show that they actually hire in even ratios: 50 percent male and 50 percent female. Yet, 80 percent of their female salespeople leave the company within the first 12 months. The attrition rate for male salespeople is about 15 percent. The CEO wants to retain good salespeople of both genders and has become concerned at the loss of dollars in recruiting and training women who leave within a year. How would you go about solving this problem?

Step 1. _____

Step 2. _____

Step 3. _____

Step 4. _____

Step 5. _____

# But on the Other Hand ...

Be Decisive

## The Skill, Trait, or Attitude

You understand the urgency in making some decisions, and do not let ambiguity about the situation and available information paralyze you. You make a firm decision in such urgent situations and set about to carry out the decision and make it the correct course of action.

## Uses on the Job

Deciding about placing an ad on an upcoming event in a key business journal before the deadline for a special edition

Deciding whether to hire a job applicant before he or she accepts another position

Deciding whether to purchase property in a fast-developing part of the city

Deciding when to invest excess capital in the stock market

Deciding whether to terminate an expensively developed marketing campaign that is generating much fewer sales leads than anticipated

Deciding whether to terminate an experienced and productive employee whose attitude negatively affects coworkers

## Run That by Me Again

At times, we fear making a wrong decision, so we make no decision at all. By avoiding the decision altogether, we rock along with the attitude that if "it isn't totally broken, don't fix it yet." Some people hesitate to make decisions without having a team or committee behind them to take the flak if things don't turn out well.

Building consensus works well, but group decisions take time—time that a specific situation may not allow. Another reason we drag our feet when faced with a decision is that we think that shedding more information on the situation will make the decision easier. Not always true. More information does not necessarily ensure a better decision.

In some situations, a wrong decision is better than no decision at all. If no decision is made, all action toward a goal may stop. Then we begin to lose momentum and even lose ground on the progress we've made so far.

At the least, a wrong decision continues to generate action. And as soon as people become aware that it's a bad decision, they go to work trying to reshape it and improve upon it. Eventually, they or you will get things back on track. Few decisions are irreversible.

Decisiveness involves the ability to recognize urgency and act without a clear-cut picture of what's ahead. When it becomes apparent that the original decisions were wrong, decisive people do not penalize themselves. They face the next decision with unshaken confidence.

## Rate Yourself

How long does it take you to decide which movie to see on the weekend?

_____ Too long          _____ Quick decision

Do you feel stressed over relatively minor decisions, like what to order from a restaurant menu or which suit to purchase?

_____ Stressed          _____ Quick decision

How long does it take you to make the smallest decisions on your job?

_____ Too long        _____ Quick decision

How do you feel about making the big decisions on your job?

_____ Stressed        _____ Confident

Can you recall three wrong decisions (from your current perspective) that you still feel okay about having made at the time you made them?

1. _____

2. _____

3. _____

# Whoever Made This Decision Needs to Be Shot

Make Quality Decisions

### The Skill, Trait, or Attitude

You recognize opportunities for and barriers to reaching your own goals or those set for you by someone else. You consider relevant facts, understand cause and effect relationships, generate and evaluate alternatives, and choose the best options to reach your goals.

### Uses on the Job

Pricing a new service or product for a new market

Hiring the best candidate for a new position

Partnering with a supplier to produce a single client solution

Deciding which market segment to penetrate with a new product

Deciding whether to give a dissatisfied client a refund on a service you have already provided

Purchasing new equipment from a profusion of choices

### Run That by Me Again

Decisions typically fall into two categories: a problem or an opportunity. We can make a decision in two ways: Decide and act, or refuse to decide and thereby let circumstances dictate the outcome. The easiest decisions are the "yes" or "no" decisions; the most difficult ones call for us to compare several alternatives and select the best.

Making quality decisions does not always mean getting all the facts. As Peter Drucker points out in *The Ef-*

*fective Executive,* we start with opinions, which are worthless until tested. Neither do facts always contribute to decision making—if we judge them irrelevant.

You have several decision-making approaches at your disposal:

*The Ben Franklin Method:* Jotting down the pros and cons, canceling out those of equal weight, and then seeing which column turns out to be the longest

*The Rating System:* Deciding on the criteria and giving each option a weighted score

*The Coin Toss:* Using some meaningless gesture of fate to make the decision

*The Checklist:* Listing the criteria and, as long as the option meets the criteria, accepting that option.

*The Logic Model:* Defining the problem, collecting information, generating alternatives, measuring alternatives, deciding, acting, and evaluating

Even with all these methods, decision making can still prove troublesome on occasion. To aid in the decision-making process, consider the following tips:

**Tips**

- Saturate your mind with facts, but realize that facts may or may not be available or relevant.
- Respect your own opinions and hunches from experience.
- Seek expert opinion. Also ask for common sense thinking from "person-on-the-street" sources.
- Don't stop generating options too soon.
- Reexamine every assumption you've made about the decision situation.
- Examine the best- and worst-case extremes of all options. Eliminate the ones that expose you to consequences you can't live with.

- Compare each alternative with your objective or goal *before* you compare options to each other.
- Consider using a group to make a decision when you need buy-in, or when you need moral support to follow through.
- Seek out people who will argue with your decision, and then listen to their reasoning.
- Give yourself permission to be wrong so that you can fully accept risks.
- Be specific about your wants and needs.
- After deciding, set about implementing, not second guessing, the decision.

## Rate Yourself

Think of a recent quality decision you've made. Did you consciously use any of the processes or tips above?

_____ None    _____ Some    _____ All

Do people tend to go around you for decisions that affect them?

_____ Rarely    _____ Occasionally    _____ Often

Do other people typically seek you out and request your help in making decisions?

_____ Rarely    _____ Occasionally    _____ Often

How often does someone else with more authority reverse your decisions?

_____ Rarely    _____ Occasionally    _____ Often

How often do you regret your own decisions?

_____ Rarely    _____ Occasionally    _____ Often

Do your decisions generally lead you to accomplish your goals?

_____ Rarely    _____ Occasionally    _____ Often

# Work Means Having to Say You're Sorry

Apologize for Mistakes
and Situations

## The Skill, Trait, or Attitude

You have a healthy self-esteem that allows you to acknowledge mistakes and express regret for them. You can also accept responsibility for situations, problems, or errors that you did not cause. You apologize with sincerity for the consequences or unfortunate circumstances that result for others.

## Uses on the Job

Apologizing to customers for errors

Empathizing with toward others in unfortunate situations or circumstances relating to your product or service

Mediating a conflict between two partners for the sake of cooperating on a project that moves you toward your goal

Apologizing to a supervisor for not performing up to acceptable standards

Apologizing to a subordinate for not giving adequate direction on a project

Apologizing to team members for failing to take an action that would have benefited the team

## Run That by Me Again

"I'm sorry for any inconvenience this may have caused you," is probably the most frequently delivered line in lieu of a real apology. That statement has become an insincere cliché uttered as a reaction to almost any and all complaints or problems, with no real acknowledgment of error and no sincere regret.

A sincere apology acknowledges a specific error, neglect, or insensitivity. Your comments demonstrate to the other person that you understand the predicament or consequences caused. Finally, an apology focuses on corrective action.

In more than one company where I've been leading business writing or customer service training, I've been told by misguided employees or managers that they never apologize. When asked to elaborate, they'll often give the explanation that apologizing is a sign of weakness. But weak people don't apologize. As Leo Buscaglia says, "Gentleness can only be expected from the strong." Other people hesitate to apologize for fear of liability issues. But again, that thinking is misguided; an apology about an unfortunate *situation* doesn't assume *responsibility* for that situation.

The long-term profit doesn't come in *winning* customers, but in *keeping* customers. People can't do business together long without either an intentional or unintentional mistake or insensitivity. Coworkers can't perform as a team for long without someone goofing up—doing or saying something they shouldn't have, or not doing or saying something they should have. An apology can be the salve that helps to heal the wound—and if it doesn't heal the wound, it mitigates the pain.

## Rate Yourself

When was the last time you voiced a sincere acknowledgment of error or insensitivity and apologized to someone?

_____

After you apologize, do people tend to let go of the situation or continue to bring it up again? (When others won't let go, that's a good sign that they didn't consider your apology sincere.)

_____ Let go     _____ Continue to bring it up

# I Don't Care What He Does as Long as He Stays out of My Way

Forgive and Refuse to Hold Grudges

## The Skill, Trait, or Attitude

You can conquer the inclination to get even when someone wrongs you. You acknowledge that another person made a real mistake or committed a wrong, but still conclude that the other person deserves love and respect. You give other people the benefit of the doubt about their intentions when their behavior, words, or actions cause you difficulty or pain. You actively work to mend broken relationships.

## Uses on the Job

Forgiving obnoxious customers for the good of the company's relationship with them

Forgiving a supervisor for belittling your work on a project, for the larger benefit of accomplishing an organizational goal

Forgiving a team member for embarrassing or hurtful comments in a meeting

Forgiving a coworker for not asking for your input on a major decision that affects you

Forgiving someone for taking credit for one of your ideas

## Run That by Me Again

The English poet Alexander Pope observed, "A brave man thinks no one his superior who does him an injury; for he has it then in his power to make himself superior to the other by forgiving it."

E. H. Chapin, an American clergyman, agrees: "Never does the human soul appear so strong and noble as when it foregoes revenge, and dares to forgive an injury."

Dr. John Gray, author of several best-selling relationship books, insists that forgiveness is a skill to be learned. Either we see our parents model it, or we don't. Some of us go through life feeling stifled by the love we have to give because we cannot forgive others for being imperfect and we cannot forgive ourselves.

Unspent anger over an insult or a mistake wastes time, decreases productivity, and increases stress on the job. Nothing produces a good night's sleep or a good day's work like releasing from your mind a wrong done to you.

## Rate Yourself

Do you dread meeting a customer in the airport or on the street because of an unresolved conflict?

_____ Yes _____ No

Have you altered a project (bypassed someone capable of giving valuable input on a decision, changed your work schedule, reassigned staff) because you still hold a grudge against someone?

_____ Yes _____ No

Have you ever withdrawn from a task force because you still hold a grudge against someone?

_____ Yes _____ No

Is there a qualified coworker that you would refuse to accept on your next project team? Why?

_____ Yes _____ No

Because: _____

Do you experience stress and turmoil in your personal life because you cannot forgive?

_____ Yes _____ No

Are you on speaking terms with all the members of your family? Are you willing to take the first step to mend a relationship?

_____ Yes _____ No

# Look, There's No Law Against It

## Be Ethical and Do the Ethical Thing

### The Skill, Trait, or Attitude

You have a high moral standard and practice moral behavior. That is, you make decisions and take actions based not necessarily on what is expedient but on a moral principle and belief system. You go beyond the letter of laws, agreements, or rules to consider what is morally right. You can withstand the pressure to take the easiest, unethical route when you are pressured to achieve results beyond your expertise or resources.

### Uses on the Job

Deciding not to award a contract to a friend or family member because that contractor is not the best qualified or does not offer the best pricing or quality

Resisting the temptation to bill your own company or client companies for unnecessary travel expenses

Refusing to bribe purchasing agents or to accept bribes for your own decisions to favor a specific supplier

Refusing to use deceptive, misleading advertising

Refusing to sell products that you know to be faulty

Respecting rather than destroying the dignity of employees

Refusing salary or payment for work not done or time not spent on productive tasks

Telling the truth about mistakes or work completed by yourself, your subordinates, and your coworkers

Resisting the temptation to access records or falsify information not authorized for your use

Speaking up with information or telling the full truth when you know facts are being misinterpreted or others are jumping to wrong conclusions

Resisting the urge to inflate information on a resume or in a proposal to win a job or project

## Run That by Me Again

Most of us understand what an ethical act or decision is. Although people have different standards about right and wrong, most standards are shared by society as a whole. At the minimum, acts and decisions should be legal. But the law sets only the *minimum* standard.

Leaders and philosophers through the ages have added to the definition of ethical behavior: 1) acts or decisions that create benefit for the most people and acts that do not infringe on basic human rights; 2) acts and decisions that over the long haul increase the self-esteem and mental health of the person engaging in the act or decision. These two screening issues alone raise the ante for ethical behavior.

A large hospital system in the Dallas-Fort Worth metroplex was the recipient of a charitable donation of property under the bargain-sale provision of the IRS guidelines. The alert and capable hospital administrator used his influence to guide the board of directors in their decision to pay the nominal price for the property and then resell the property and put the cash into its cancer research program.

About two months after acquiring the property, the brother of the hospital administrator came for a visit, saw the property, and decided that it would be perfect for his purposes. The logical and legal decision would have been for the hospital to resell the property to the visiting brother. However, the hospital administrator held to a higher moral principle, refusing to allow a family member to benefit from the bargain-priced donation of land.

A 1995 study by the Association of Certified Fraud Examiners, an Austin trade group, estimates employee crime costs employers a stunning $400 billion dollars annually (almost four times the level in the late 1980s). Honesty is no longer a "given" among customers or employees.

Ethical decisions may not make sense in any given situation, but that makes them no less right. A moral principle stands as a permanent guide in temporary situations.

## Rate Yourself

Would you be worried or embarrassed if you suddenly learned that your every action and decision of the past five years had been videotaped for viewing by your employer and your family?

_____ Worried and embarrassed     _____ At peace

# Something Came Up

Be Dependable

## The Skill, Trait, or Attitude

If you are responsible, you take charge. Not only are you responsible for things you control, but when invited, you shoulder responsibility for situations under others' direct control. If you start something, you finish it. If you promise, you deliver.

## Uses on the Job

Completing a project on time and with the available resources, despite obstacles and difficulties blocking your path toward the goal

Putting aside personal inconveniences when asked to attend key team meetings

Participating in extracurricular activities with a client just to show interest, even when your supervisor hasn't definitely asked you to be present

Looking out for the well-being of your coworkers, even when not specifically asked to do something special for them

Pulling your weight on team projects, even when you have the opportunity to "hide" without accepting personal responsibilities and tasks

Volunteering to help on a project, even though the timing isn't best for you

## Run That by Me Again

"Flash powder makes a more brilliant light than the arc lamp, but you cannot use it to light your street corner because it doesn't last long enough. Stability is more essential to success than brilliancy." (Taken from *Rotograph*.)

Our literature is full of such analogies and parables, from Aesop's fable of the tortoise and the hare to the legend of the little Dutch boy holding his finger in the dike to save the city. Creative, bright people swarm around the scene of action. But they often disappear when problems develop, when more exciting projects surface, or when things become more work than fun.

Most employers would agree that for long-term success you need people who assume responsibility and stay around to deal with the consequences of decisions and plans.

## Rate Yourself

Do you frequently "lose interest" in projects that run into difficulties?

_____ Lose interest    _____ Persevere

How often do you delay in taking action until someone reminds you with a call, memo, or e-mail?

_____ Delay    _____ Follow through without prompts

Is your word your bond? Do people frequently ask you to put it in writing before they'll accept your decisions or work?

_____ Change my mind    _____ Keep my word

Are you generally the first person or the last person to leave the scene of difficult work?

_____ First    _____ Last

# Just Say the Word

Take Initiative

## The Skill, Trait, or Attitude

You do not wait to be told what to do. You are observant of what goes on around you. You learn new skills without waiting for someone to send you to training. You ask the *why* behind things. You pay attention to trends, issues, and new challenges so that you can take advantage of early opportunities and can plan to prevent problems.

## Uses on the Job

Assuming a new job for which all the parameters haven't been set or reshaping a job to handle more responsibilities

Meeting a client's need before the client has explicitly asked

Finding a way to save money before anyone has complained about expenses

Improving a process before anyone has complained that the process is inefficient or difficult

"Owning" a problem from beginning to end

## Run That by Me Again

The lowest level of initiative is waiting to be told what to do. A step up is asking what you can do. The third level is recommending things to be done that you see as particularly helpful, profitable, or effective. Fourth is acting and then telling your boss immediately after what you've done, in time for him or her to undo it if necessary. The highest level of initiative is to take action and then report what you've done at some later time.

Certainly, you can't take the same level of initiative in all tasks, problems, or assignments because the potential for disaster varies from situation to situation. But you can make it a habit to look for problems you can solve, accept challenges you can meet, or do tasks and jobs that no one else wants to do.

A decade ago, before starting a new task, employees and bosses discussed it, planned it, and trained for it. But in today's fast-paced world, if you have to wait to be told what to do next and how to do it, you're standing still in a relay race. Those who expect to receive the baton are running alongside the leader, waiting for the hand-off. If you're standing still waiting for someone to give you your next assignment, your doing it may be pointless and your contribution valueless.

## Rate Yourself

How many processes have you improved since you've been in your current job?

_____ None _____ A few _____ Many

When you present a problem to someone, do you also typically present possible solutions?

_____ Problem only _____ Solutions

Suppose a coworker or staff member brings to your attention an unusual, promising idea, but expresses concern that no one else is doing things that way. Would your typical response be "Let's wait and see" or "Let's try it"?

_____ Wait _____ Try it

Consider how many "firsts" you have on your work record. (Example: First person in the department/division/company/industry to ...)

1. _____

2. _____

3. _____

# What Are My Odds?

Take Calculated Risks

## The Skill, Trait, or Attitude

You place yourself in challenging situations where you must make a decision or take action that exposes you or others to loss, damage, or injury. You accurately assess a situation (both its rewards and its consequences) and do not let *fear* of making the wrong decision or taking the wrong action paralyze you into indecision or inaction.

## Uses on the Job

Deciding to fund an expensive, untested marketing campaign

Funding a research project for a new product

Contradicting a client about organizational needs and making recommendations you know the client will initially oppose

Risking your reputation by accepting an assignment for which you've had little or no previous experience

Running for office in your professional organization

## Run That by Me Again

One of the most well-known admonitions about risk taking is the biblical Parable of the Talents. The master of the household gives five talents to one steward; that steward invests the money and returns ten talents to the master. Likewise, the steward given two talents by the master invests his money and returns four talents to the master. Both the five-talent and the two-talent stewards win accolades for their risk taking. But the steward who receives only one talent buries his, for fear of losing all in the marketplace. The displeased master chastises the third steward for his failure to take a risk.

Far too many people are burying their ideas and potential for gain in the marketplace. They lack the courage to grow. But they fail to realize that remaining stagnant in their careers carries the risk of ultimate failure.

As William Bennett points out in his *Book of Virtues,* the novelist Herman Melville makes a clear distinction between fear and risk. In the classic *Moby Dick,* Starbuck, the chief mate of the *Pequod,* tells his crew, "I will have no man in my boat who is not afraid of a whale." With this pronouncement, he seemed to mean that reckless abandon was not the ticket. Instead, he wanted sailors who calculated the risk and understood the peril they faced. Unfearful sailors posed the greatest danger of doing stupid things.

On the job, we don't need fools who rush into projects and decisions without understanding the cost of a mistake. Instead, we need people who accurately estimate the rewards and consequences of a particular decision. If the risk seems likely to pay off, they act with courage for the potential gain even though they may be fearful of the consequences.

Aristotle wrote in *The Nicomachean Ethics,* "We become brave by doing braving acts." Interim failures become the research that leads to eventual success.

## Rate Yourself

When faced with a risky choice in an area where you generally have total responsibility, do you make the hard decision or defer to your boss for the final go-ahead?

_____ Decide     _____ Wait for go-ahead

Suppose we could convert all risk-taking analysis to a simple chart like the one below. Circle the odds you seek before you make a risky decision:

10% chance of reward; 90% chance of consequences

20% chance of reward; 80% chance of consequences

30% chance of reward; 70% chance of consequences

40% chance of reward; 60% chance of consequences
50% chance of reward; 50% chance of consequences
60% chance of reward; 40% chance of consequences
70% chance of reward; 30% chance of consequences
80% chance of reward; 20% chance of consequences
90% chance of reward; 10% chance of consequences

List the brave acts, the risks, you have taken in the last year on the job.

1. _____
2. _____
3. _____

List the brave acts, the risks, you have taken in your personal life choices.

1. _____
2. _____
3. _____

# It's Heads You Win, Tails I Lose

Accept Ambiguity

## The Skill, Trait, or Attitude

You can function in an environment where things fluctuate outside the norms, where all the information you would like to have to make a decision is not available, where all the objectives are not clearly stated, where all the policies and procedures are not clearly detailed in writing.

## Uses on the Job

Handling a disciplinary problem with an employee when all the facts are unascertainable

Putting your heart and mind into a planning project before you know whether you'll receive final approval to proceed

Preparing contingency plans for solving a customer problem when you don't know whether your organization's new product will be ready by the time that customer needs a solution in place

Consulting with coworkers from other divisions to solve a problem when these coworkers define the problem differently

Hiring an employee when reference checks produce both positive and negative opinions about past performance

Selecting a vendor when reference checks on past projects produce both satisfied and dissatisfied previous customers

Electing to provide services for a new company, although you've received mixed information about the company's creditworthiness

## Run That by Me Again

Toleration of ambiguity is a mind-set that keeps you calm in a sea of conflicting circumstances, opinions, and information. You trust that clarity will eventually prevail, and, therefore, you don't lose patience with yourself or others in trying to decide or act. In the absence of logic and proven guidelines, you develop additional creative solutions and depend on your intuition for guidance.

## Rate Yourself

Do you frequently seek precedents for situations you're handling and feel panic when you realize you're facing uncharted waters?

_____ Feel panic     _____ Feel confident

Do you feel angry when people don't give a clear "yes" or "no" answer?

_____ Feel angry     _____ Accept ambiguity

When you discover there are no existing guidelines for a situation you're facing, do you feel freedom or alarm?

_____ Alarm     _____ Freedom

# I Can't Get My Mind off Yesterday

Focus and Concentrate

### The Skill, Trait, or Attitude

You do not become easily distracted from your primary goals and projects. You understand the difference between the urgent and the important, and you spend your time and your emotional energy accordingly. You do not let little things nag at you and dilute your passionate commitment to your most important duties and opportunities.

### Uses on the Job

Scheduling your time each day and week

Devoting your resources (money, time, people) to the highest priority projects

Writing an important report rather than taking incoming calls

Scheduling a two-day strategic planning meeting for a major project while you have several loose ends to complete by the end of the month

Giving your full attention in a meeting without arriving late, leaving early, or returning phone calls in the middle

Reaching your goal to make a certain number of outbound sales calls before you do less important activities

Planning a visit to a field office and then refusing to worry about less important issues that come up at headquarters while you're away

### Run That by Me Again

Americans have a strong penchant for doing two things at once: We carry a Walkman to listen to self-improvement tapes while we jog for exercise. We choose one-handed foods like corny dogs, chicken fingers, and ice cream cones so we can eat while we sightsee. We have pharmacies in the supermarket so we can have our prescriptions filled while we buy dinner. We have e-mail and voice mail so we can receive messages while we sleep.

For trivial matters, this two-for-one arrangement works fine. Flitting like a fly on the wall from one task to another without completing either stalls progress and creates uncertainties. Important issues demand focus and best efforts.

People often ask about the toughest group I have to handle as a consultant and trainer. They're frequently surprised at my response: The most difficult groups to keep focused are lower-level professionals and middle managers who keep dashing in and out of a session to put out fires back in their offices.

Executive groups, on the other hand, once they clear their calendars and convene to solve a problem, learn a new skill, or tackle a new challenge, concentrate on the issue at hand. They do not easily become sidetracked personally or as a group.

In one particular session I was leading, an administrative assistant with a solemn face brought in a phone message to her executive vice president. He held the message until 90 minutes later when we took a break, and then announced that their colleague (another senior executive not in attendance) had just dropped dead of a heart attack.

Executives tend to bring focus to every facet of their job; concentration is the key to their ongoing success.

Webster defines *concentration* to mean "to gather together, to make stronger, to fix one's attention." Contrast its opposite, *dilute*: "to make weaker by mixing with something else." Executives make strong decisions by focusing on their primary goal and concentrating on information and situations leading to that goal.

## Rate Yourself

Do you habitually plan uninterrupted time for planning or thinking about key projects?

_____ Yes _____ No

Do you have an open-door policy that encourages unnecessary interruptions and makes concentration difficult?

_____ Open door _____ Scheduled quiet time

Do you associate your most important projects or tasks with a certain schedule and site? That is, do you have a same-time, same-place habit of forcing yourself to work on lengthy, complex projects?

_____ Yes _____ No

Do you work and break by the clock, or if you're on a roll, do you typically stay with a task until completion?

_____ Break by the clock _____ Stay with it

At the end of a month, do you feel as though you have started many projects and completed none?

_____ Feel unfinished _____ Feel satisfied
                                         with completions

# How Much Farther, Daddy?

Persevere

## The Skill, Trait, or Attitude

You motivate yourself to persist in the face of difficult circumstances and unfavorable odds. You demonstrate commitment long after others give up on making an idea work or reaching a goal.

## Uses on the Job

Completing tedious tasks and projects

Continuing to research, document, refine, and reshape ideas and present them to others for approval even when they've already rejected your idea in its initial stages

Researching a solution to a long-standing problem

Searching for a cure to a health problem

Continuing to encourage and train a willing employee over a long period of time to improve performance to an acceptable standard

Calling that potential customer six times because you know the average salesperson stops at five calls

## Run That by Me Again

Calvin Coolidge observed, "Nothing in the world can take the place of persistence. Talent will not; nothing is more common than unsuccessful men with talent. Genius will not; unrewarded genius is almost a proverb. Education will not; the world is full of educated derelicts. Persistence and determination alone are omnipotent."

People who really want to do something give it their all; the less determined give an excuse. Napoleon Hill concluded, "The majority of men meet with failure because of their lack of persistence in creating new plans to take the place of those which fail."

Consider how many people have been inches away from success because they gave up too soon. In your own life, recall activities you've tried, skills you've attempted to master, ideas you've dreamed about pursuing. How do you know that you didn't stop just short of success? A few people may succeed because they are destined to, but most people succeed because they are determined to.

## Rate Yourself

List any projects you've been actively trying to complete or any goal you've been actively striving to achieve in the face of difficult circumstances over the last five-year period:

1. _____

2. _____

3. _____

What is your current state of mind about each of these goals or projects? Write the corresponding letter below beside each project listed above:

**a.** It's dead. It can't be done.

**b.** I'll probably get back to it someday.

**c.** It's something worth working on, but I'm no longer going to kill myself to do it.

**d.** I'm working on a back-up, alternative plan just now and getting there by inches.

**e.** I will do it—it's only a matter of time.

# You Want It Fried, Stuffed, Grilled, Baked, Broiled, or Blackened?

Accommodate Change; Be Flexible

### The Skill, Trait, or Attitude

Your mind and emotions do not flinch with the prospect of change. You are flexible enough to apply your skills, commitment, and energy to any number of tasks or responsibilities. You face new circumstances with an open mind. Change excites and challenges you.

### Uses on the Job

Adapting to new human resource policies about flextime, vacation time, holidays, unpaid leave, and so forth

Learning to sell your product or service over the phone versus face to face

Switching from a direct sales force to distributors selling your product

Moving from one location to another and adapting to a workspace of a different size

Using new equipment to accomplish tasks formerly handled manually

Changing your computer platform for all software applications

Working with a new supervisor, team, or staff

### So Why Should I Care?

To understand change, think specifics. Do you remember when preparing a letter by typewriter was acceptable?

Then we had a taste of correcting Selectrics and couldn't go back to the old carbon copies and onion skin. Now, who prepares a letter without a computer?

Or trace the trends in shopping: from Sears mail-order catalogues, to the single retail store, to the huge shopping mall, back to the convenience of home shopping via direct mail or the Internet.

Or consider the trends in communication: Remember when it was okay to mail something that took four days to reach its destination? Remember when official signatures had to be on the original paper, rather than on a fax?

Every business product, service, or process leaves change in its wake—that is, if it endures and continues to be successful. The accelerated pace of change, however, is what keeps heads spinning. We hardly get a piece of software installed before the next version hits the street. We just barely come to understand what our supervisor expects in our status reports when the organization restructures and we inherit a new boss. We plan a new project, solicit bidders, and design the specs only to have someone cancel the funding before the project gets off the ground.

But remember that change is the gateway to progress. When faced with change:

- Think clearly and act calmly.
- Consider what you can change within yourself to best accommodate the exterior change.
- Try to recast any negative change to a positive goal.
- Direct passive fear into active energy on projects required to make the change.

People who habitually resist change become labeled and limited as losers.

## Rate Yourself

Check your typical attitude about change against the following specifics:

| | Hate It | OK, Once I'm Used to It | Welcome It! |
|---|---|---|---|
| New breakfast cereal | _____ | _____ | _____ |
| New menu in favorite restaurant | _____ | _____ | _____ |
| New departure time for weekly flight | _____ | _____ | _____ |
| New officers in civic association | _____ | _____ | _____ |
| New day for staff meeting | _____ | _____ | _____ |
| New way to answer the telephone | _____ | _____ | _____ |
| New software | _____ | _____ | _____ |
| New procedure for key project | _____ | _____ | _____ |
| New performance measurement | _____ | _____ | _____ |
| New bonus plan | _____ | _____ | _____ |
| New healthcare plan | _____ | _____ | _____ |
| New coworker | _____ | _____ | _____ |
| New boss or employer | _____ | _____ | _____ |
| New service | _____ | _____ | _____ |

# When's School Out? Whatever Happened to Summer Vacations?

Learn to Learn

## The Skill, Trait, or Attitude

You have the mental capacity and the willingness to learn new things. You recognize when you need more skills or knowledge to do an excellent job and identify appropriate sources for training or information. You are willing to seek new information, model others with more skill, practice the skill or study the information until you have mastered it, and then apply that skill or information to your area of responsibility. Finally, you demonstrate and document your new expertise.

## Uses on the Job

Learning a new software package

Designing new product packaging to take advantage of lower cost on raw materials

Testing chemical reactions with a new instrument

Accessing information in a new filing system

Changing the way you give performance feedback to members of your staff or team

Beginning a new line of business in a new industry

## So Why Should I Care?

"What is life all about? Development, growth. The two great laws of life are growth and decay. When things stop growing, they begin to die. This is true of men, business, or nations," observed Charles Gow.

Learning is what the average person will do most of the workday in the twenty-first century. Those unwilling to learn become deadwood—the people who have stopped working but stay on the payroll and complicate things for people who have to go around them to get the job done.

Anyone who cannot or will not learn cannot be a long-term employee in today's workplace. The pace of change will overtake them in most jobs.

## Tips

Take advantage of any of the following ways to continue your professional growth:

Apprenticeships on the job; one-on-one coaching

Self-study items such as books, videos, audios, interactive software, or CDs

Benchmarking with other organizations or star performers

Distance-learning courses offered via computer or satellite

Certification programs through your professional organization

Field trips

Attendance at symposiums, conventions, or trade shows sponsored by your professional organization

Reading journals and magazines

User manuals (policies, procedures, operations, specs)

Attending lectures or programs at universities or community colleges

Training courses formally established by your organization or available from outside vendors

Learning your own customers' or suppliers' database, certification, training

Networking with people above your skill level

## Rate Yourself

When was the last time you completed a training program? _____

List the job-related books you've read in the last six months:

1. _____

2. _____

3. _____

4. _____

What industry or business journals do you read regularly?

_____

How often do you meet with your coach or mentor about current projects or career plans?

_____ Monthly      _____ Quarterly      _____ Annually

What new skill or knowledge have you applied to your job in the last month? _____

# May I Help You with Something?

Develop a Service Attitude

## The Skill, Trait, or Attitude

You gain great satisfaction from serving others: customers, colleagues, or coworkers. You are responsive, reassuring, empathetic, consistent, and honest with them. You eagerly try to make a contribution to their lives. You are willing to make things better without receiving credit for your actions.

## Uses on the Job

Managing people

Setting policy for your organization

Serving customers

Participating in community affairs and boards as a representative of your organization

Leading or participating on a project team

## Run That by Me Again

Servant *leadership* has become a ubiquitous term in the last few years in books by CEOs, in the teaching and writing of university professors, and in the speeches of motivational heroes. Truett Cathy, founder of Chick-fil-A and a prime proponent of servant leadership, insists that his corporate goal has been the desire to contribute to the well-being of anyone who comes into contact with the business. Other CEOs like him measure their net worth in contributions to society rather than the acquisition of stock.

Servant *followship* hasn't received as much attention. People follow leaders, but often for their own reasons. In a customer service workshop for a large airline client, our discussion turned to internal versus external customers. Someone remarked that instead of getting along with coworkers as one big happy family they routinely acted as squabbling siblings. I'm afraid that's true for many organizations.

Ask customer service managers what constitutes excellent customer service, and their list would look like this: reliability, responsiveness, a reassuring tone and manner, empathy about negative situations, product or service knowledge, honesty, progress reports about action being taken, clear instructions, apologies for errors, problem resolution, and appreciation for their business. Which of those isn't appropriate for our own coworkers and colleagues?

But instead of an I'm-here-to-serve-you attitude with coworkers and customers, people often adopt these dispositions:

- Just hold on, will you? What's your hurry? I'll do it when I get good and ready.
- Because it's important to you, doesn't mean it's important to me.
- Hurry up and wait for me.
- I don't care what you do/know/think.
- I've got the truth. You don't.
- I'm running this place, not you.
- Where does it say that I have to do that?
- You don't like it? So what are you going to do about it?
- Make me care.

A service attitude shows a commitment to "make it happen" for the other person without concern for reward for yourself.

## Rate Yourself

How often do you alter your schedule to accommodate someone else's schedule—when you have nothing to gain?

_____ Rarely _____ Sometimes _____ Often

Do you answer questions with a helpful or tolerant tone?

_____ Tolerant _____ Helpful

How often do you exceed your job description to accommodate another employee of your organization?

_____ Rarely _____ Sometimes _____ Often

How many new customers (or how much increased business from long-term customers) could your organization trace to your own service efforts?

_____ Not much _____ Some _____ A great deal

For you, is customer service an attitude or a department?

_____ Attitude _____ Department

# I'm Not Goin' Down for You, Man!

Nurture Personal Relationships

### The Skill, Trait, or Attitude

You build personal relationships easily. Understanding their value, you network with others at work and in the community to discover commonalities. You share time, trade information, demonstrate concern, build goodwill, and gain satisfaction from interacting with others.

### Uses on the Job

Gaining informal support for your controversial idea or project

Mediating and resolving conflicts between coworkers

Shaping public impressions about your organization

Gaining opinions and information (about competitors, customers, and the general market) to do your job better

### Run That by Me Again

For the past 17 years, our communication training company has focused primarily on teaching people to write well (proposals, reports, manuals, letters, memos, e-mail) and speak well (presentations to customers, internal decision makers, civic groups, the public). However, about four years ago, we began to develop customer service and other interpersonal skills courses because of calls from clients with comments like this one from a high-tech firm:

Can you help our system engineers with basic one-on-one, face-to-face communication? These people have extensive experience and expertise in designing computer solutions. But they have difficulty interacting comfortably with the executive decision makers when they're at the customer site. They've been sitting behind a computer so long that they have trouble carrying on a real conversation with a live person.

Like muscles, communication skills atrophy from lack of use. And communication skills suffer for lack of networking opportunities. Our inability to establish rapport with coworkers and customers is a direct reflection of our growing physical isolation.

Decades ago, we bumped into people without really trying—on the sidewalk, in the neighborhood theater, in the football stadium, in the shopping mall, at the annual convention. Today, we use mass transit with cars full of strangers, rent video movies for home, play computer games rather than two-below football, shop by mail or Internet, and "attend" meetings via conference calls or satellite. Many of us have not met those living next door or across the street.

Our personal and professional relationships grow weaker or stronger in direct proportion to our skill, commitment, and intensity in maintaining them. Technology has provided ways for people to stay in touch 24 hours a day. But nurturing a relationship is what happens beyond the exchange of useful information.

## Rate Yourself

Count the relationships (customers, coworkers, suppliers, industry and community colleagues) you've developed as a part of your activity in the workplace and in the community.

____ Fewer than 10 ____ 11–30 ____ 31–100 ____ 100 or more

How many of these people do you talk with more often than once a month?    _____

How many of them do you know well enough to know what they enjoy as a pastime or hobby? _____

How many do you consider casual friends? _____

How many of them would you ask for a suggestion about handling cranky coworker? _____

How many would you call if your parent or child died? _____

# I Hate Cocktail Parties

Practice Proper Etiquette

## The Skill, Trait, or Attitude

You know the social rules of business interactions such as making introductions, dining as a guest, hosting functions, traveling with coworkers and customers, grooming, gift giving, telephoning, and meeting and greeting. You also understand which of these social or business rituals varies from culture to culture and know the importance of researching the customs of any particular group with which you interact. Before traveling internationally, you learn the cultural practices of your host.

## Uses on the Job

Selling your product or service domestically and globally

Setting appointments and greeting colleagues

Traveling to set up a branch office in another country

Screening, hiring, and training job applicants from cultures other than your own

Attending or hosting a meal function for a group of customers, coworkers, and colleagues

## So Why Should I Care?

Let me share three incidents involving proper etiquette that made a difference in either gaining business or determining the promotability of an individual:

A large high-tech firm recently hosted a $100,000 social function to allow representatives of a potential client organization get to know its own staff who would be designing and supporting their computer solutions. The company handpicked a team of managers to fly across country to mix and mingle as hosts for this two-day event. The potential contract at stake amounted to $500 million.

A second situation: The director of human resources at a large financial institution broke the news to a senior manager that he would not receive the promotion to senior vice president. As the message bearer discussed the decision with me before breaking the news to the manager, he shared this explanation: "Robert's gone as far as he'll go. He has been passed over for promotion because he just doesn't understand the finer points of socializing with executives. He always looks a little disheveled with a twig of hair that hangs down over his forehead and his tie is always a little too loose. At social get-togethers, he and his wife just don't know how to carry on a conversation without being gauche."

A third incident: Our in-country sponsor in Malaysia arranged for a company representative of the client firm to meet my husband and me at the airport as we traveled there for speaking engagements and consulting work. After arranging for our baggage to be loaded into the trunk, our Malaysian greeter gestured toward the passenger side of his car as he headed around for the driver's seat. I slid into the back seat, and my husband spontaneously crawled into the back seat beside me for the half-hour trip to our hotel.

The man suddenly grew quiet. He answered our questions only minimally and volunteered no information about himself or the company at all. The next day at the client site with our sponsor, we learned that the man who had met us at the airport was our client contact, the manager of human resources. For the next 10 days while we worked with his organization, all of our other contacts with that organization were very cordial and complimentary of our work with them. But this manager remained aloof and performed only the perfunctory kindnesses.

Finally, perplexed and perturbed at ourselves because we couldn't seem to turn the situation around, we asked our sponsor to investigate whether we had somehow offended this man. Yes, our sponsor reported back to us. When my husband had seated himself in the back seat with me rather than up front, the client had interpreted my husband's action to be demeaning, inferring that we considered him a hired driver.

His was the only company with which we did not get repeat business.

With more and more people having identical technical skills and academic credentials, social interactions take on increasing importance for winning a project or losing a project, landing a job, and keeping a job.

## Rate Yourself

Do you know in which order to call names when introducing a junior person to a more senior person?

_____ Yes _____ No

Can you identify which types of gifts would be inappropriate to give to someone on your support staff team?

_____ Yes _____ No

Do you know whether you should handwrite or type a condolence message to a colleague?

_____ Yes _____ No

Do you know what to do with your table napkin at the conclusion of a meal?

_____ Yes _____ No

Do you know in which countries it is inappropriate to write on the back of a business card handed to you when meeting with a business contact?

_____ Yes _____ No

# I Fall to Pieces Every Time You Call My Name; I'm Not Stressed—I Always Yell Like This

Maintain Emotional Equilibrium;
Control Stress

### The Skill, Trait, or Attitude

You keep your emotions under control. You can express anger, hurt, disappointment, embarrassment, or excitement in appropriate ways in appropriate settings. You don't fly off the handle or lose your composure unexpectedly. Under stress, you do not make rash decisions or take hasty action that will produce damaging consequences you'll later regret.

### Uses on the Job

Refraining from raising your voice and using an impatient tone with an unhappy customer

Holding back a bitter retort when someone gives you negative feedback

Straining impatience from your tone when a coworker asks you to repeat simple instructions

Holding back tears of hurt or embarrassment when a team member makes a belittling remark to you in front of others in a meeting

Performing your assigned tasks in a consistent, dependable manner

## Elaboration

Stress plays havoc with our emotions. When angry, we may curse or attempt to punch someone out. When feeling playful, we may laugh boorishly loudly or giggle like a child. When we feel insulted or slighted, we may cry or pout. When tired or overwhelmed, we may burst into tears, yell, or sit passively staring at the wall. None of these emotional outbursts or states creates friends among coworkers or impresses customers positively.

Most workplaces are more relaxed than they were even five or ten years ago. We have casual-dress days, stretch our creative muscles while using paper airplanes to come up with new product designs, and play games like Marooned on a Desert Island in training courses.

But the waitress doesn't tell you about her recent knee surgery when she brings the entree. The ticket-taker at the movie theater doesn't cry and tell you about his divorce as you walk in to see the latest drama. Nor does the lawyer mention that her own house is in foreclosure proceedings while she's preparing your will. Even celebrity football players get fined and have to sit out games for their temper tantrums on the field.

That's not to say that we can't discuss personal problems and show feelings with work friends. But it does mean being in control and using proper judgment when such personal talk is inappropriate.

## Importance on the Job

In its June 1996 issue, *HR Magazine* focused on workplace violence in more than 100 of the nation's largest companies: Thirty percent reported deaths from workplace violence in the past five years. More than 70 percent reported an average of 18 minor injuries, and 66 percent reported an average of 31 incidents of minor property damage from workplace violence.

The lack of self-control is not a *new* problem created by an unfriendly, fast-changing workplace. Consider these two biblical proverbs: "A person without self-control is as defenseless as a city with broken-down walls," and "It is better to have self-control than to control an army."

Coworkers with an important customer or executive in tow try to avoid creating scenes with someone who acts and reacts unpredictably. Instead, fearing an outburst by an emotionally unbalanced person, they skirt difficult issues, withhold important information, reassign sensitive projects, and avoid him or her socially.

Uncontrolled emotion can alienate people, prevent personal achievement and growth, and harm your physical health.

## Rate Yourself

Have you ever yelled at a coworker or customer?

_____ Yes  _____ No

Do you pout and withdraw when you don't get your way?

_____ Yes  _____ No

Do you use poor-me tirades and tears to gain sympathy?

_____ Yes  _____ No

Has anyone ever called an unexpected break or dismissed a meeting when you were visibly angry?

_____ Yes  _____ No

Do subordinates seem spiritless when you tell them to do something difficult or unpleasant?

_____ Yes  _____ No

Do people seem to feel free to disagree with you or challenge something you've said? Do people give in to you often and unexpectedly?

_____ Give in  _____ Feel free to disagree

# I'd Rather Just Eat Soul Food

Balance Personal, Family, and Business
Priorities; Develop Your Spiritual Nature

## The Skill, Trait, or Attitude

You live a well-rounded life. You mix personal, family, and business activities to promote good mental and physical health. You combine both the physical and spiritual dimensions in your daily life.

## Uses on the Job

Taking time off from work for important family events

Scheduling and taking vacations and holidays for personal rest and relaxation

Sharing work accomplishments and disappointments with family and friends

Sharing personal and family triumphs and joys with business associates

Finding a job that you love—that allows you to combine personal pursuits and passions with your work

## Run That by Me Again

You understand that there is more to life than the physical. You do not mistake building a bank account with building a life. Peter Senge, writing in *The Fifth Discipline* about learning organizations and the people who thrive in them, has this to say: "People with a high level of personal mastery share several basic characteristics. They have a special sense of purpose that lies behind their visions and goals. *For such a person, a vision is a calling rather than simply a good idea.*"

Why do organizations care if their employees experience personal balance in life? When people feel comfortable with their personal purpose, they can care about others. When people genuinely care about others, they care about what they do and how their actions affect others. They are eager to come to work each day and to go home each evening. They have emotional support from family and friends that helps them deal with frustrations and obstacles at work. Because they care about what they do at work, they do it with commitment and passion. The closer their jobs align with their personal pleasures and priorities, the more fulfillment they'll feel in doing their jobs.

But an overcommitment to work, particularly work that doesn't incorporate personal interests and goals, ultimately leads to dissatisfaction on the job. If we let work become our whole existence, then the expectations that we hold about our jobs will prove to be totally unrealistic. If we invest our total selves at work, we'll come to expect total fulfillment from the job. Eventually, our relationships will break down and our spirits will starve.

A job applicant sat in my office a few days ago. As usual, I questioned her about her reason for seeking a job change. She summarized it like this:

> You'll notice I worked for Texaco for seven years and got my MBA in night school. I graduated on a Friday night and moved to San Antonio over the weekend to begin a new job with a consulting firm. The first project I joined was a turnaround operation. Twenty-two surgery centers were on the verge of bankruptcy, and 36 months later, we had made them all profitable enough to sell. It was the most exciting three years of my life, but I worked seven days a week, 12 to 14 hours a day. Then within another week, I started as sales and marketing manager for a retailer, traveling over a seven-state region. Retailers work seven days a week so I had to be available to them on Saturdays and Sundays. But when they took Tuesday or Wednesday as their day off, I

couldn't. Another store needed me. So why am I now wanting to change jobs? I want to take my life back!

The workplace needs whole individuals.

## Rate Yourself

When was the last time you took off two hours in the middle of the day to spend time with a friend or family member for no reason?      _____

How often do you schedule vacation days?      _____

Does your family resent your work? Do you seem to have more and more conflict at home about work priorities?

_____ Yes      _____ No

Do you routinely schedule time for personal pursuits— aside from family and business activities?

_____ Yes      _____ No

How often do you play?

_____ Rarely      _____ Often

Are you content at your job?

_____ Yes      _____ No

# Do You See What I See?

Present Your Expertise Internally and Externally

## The Skill, Trait, or Attitude

You have the ability to sell yourself. You can articulate both verbally and in writing your skills, experience, and accomplishments so that others understand and have confidence in your expertise. You continually document your expertise in teamwork projects, coaching, consulting, publishing, and recognition from your organization and industry.

## Uses on the Job

Mentoring coworkers and colleagues

Gaining requested transfers to new positions within your organization

Asking for and accepting more responsibilities within your organization

Winning customer business through effective proposals and oral presentations

Performing consulting contracts and leading customers to accept your research and adopt your ideas

Generating confidence among your team members because you are on the team

## So Why Should I Care?

What you *say* about what you know counts more than what you know. Communication skills give job candidates the edge, according to a 1996 study conducted by the National Association of Colleges and Employers (NACE). Yes, employers are still searching for well-rounded candidates with related work experience. But the top three criteria cited by employers were oral communication skills, interpersonal skills, and teamwork skills. This proved true even among the top technical and consulting firms, where those communication skills were preferred over the more transitory technical skills.

People who've been in the job force for awhile find these skills equally important in reselling their expertise every time a new position becomes available or the job requirements change. If you do your job behind the scenes—even an excellent job—without others understanding the value of what you do, you will not be rewarded appropriately.

So what's the value of establishing and documenting your expertise? First, it brings in business for your company. Several years ago, *Inc.* magazine ran a story about the actual dollar value attached to references to a company's performance in a national newspaper or magazine. These references about a key project or a product or service carry an actual dollar amount (ranging from approximately $8,000 to $22,000.) Those figures compare favorably to the fees charged by PR firms to get the same placement in the media. There's an enormous difference between that independent, third-party endorsement of your product or service versus the same claims made in your own brochure.

Second, as either an employee or an independent contractor, you'll more likely earn what you're worth.

Money and promotions aside, if you intend to get your budget approved, recommendations adopted, and improvements made in almost any job, you must continually sell your ideas and expertise.

## Tips

For quite some time, I've been making this point about establishing your expertise in a presentation titled "The No-Marketing Marketing Plan." The presentation outlines a career plan for establishing your expertise in any given arena. Here are the key steps:

- Aim to know all there is to know about a given subject.
- Identify the gurus in your field and research and read everything they've written about the subject.
- Interview the gurus and write articles based on your research, citing these experts as your sources.
- Begin a closer examination of the ideas of these experts. Compare and contrast their ideas and work, and then draw your own conclusions about the validity of their ideas and convergent views. Then identify gaps where you can add to the body of knowledge.
- Publish articles on this research about how the gurus agree and disagree, establishing yourself as an expert about the experts.
- Volunteer for internal projects that provide an opportunity to work closely with these ideas and conduct your own research about what works and what doesn't. Look for things to improve.
- Network with others who share similar interests. Make them aware of your continual research so that they funnel projects and information to you.
- Create your own model, product, or service from the expertise you've gained from your study of the best minds.
- Give your knowledge away. Publish articles and books on your subject, speak to other groups within your industry, and coach others beginning in the field.

Somewhere along the way, you will become known as an expert in your field.

## Rate Yourself

How many of your ideas have been accepted and incorporated into the workings of your department? Your organization?

_____ Few          _____ Some          _____ Many

How often do others outside your own work area call you to ask for your expertise and help?

_____ Rarely     _____ Sometimes     _____ Often

How many times have you been asked to represent your department in meetings with visiting dignitaries, stockholders, or representatives wanting to benchmark with your company?

_____ Rarely     _____ Sometimes     _____ Often

How often do you receive calls from outside your organization as a result of someone's referring you and your expertise on any given subject?

_____ Rarely     _____ Sometimes     _____ Often

# Bibliography

Andersen, Richard. *Getting Ahead: Career Skills for Everyone.* New York: McGraw-Hill, 1995.

Aubrey, Charles A., and Felkins, Patricia K. *Teamwork: Involving People in Quality and Productivity Improvement.* Milwaukee: The Quality Press, 1988.

Aylesworth, Thomas G., and Reagan, Gerald M. *Teaching for Thinking.* New York: Doubleday, 1969.

Baber, Anne, and Waymon, Lynne. *How to Fireproof Your Career: Survival Strategies for Volatile Times.* New York: Berkeley Books, 1995.

Bangs, David H. Jr. *Financial Troubleshooting.* Dover, NH: Upstart Publishing Company, 1992.

Bennett, William J. *The Moral Compass: Stories for a Life's Journey.* New York: Simon & Schuster, 1995.

Bennis, Warren. *On Becoming a Leader.* Reading, MA: Addison-Wesley Publishing, 1989.

Berry, Leonard L. *On Great Service: A Framework for Action.* New York: The Free Press, 1995.

Betof, Edward, and Harwood, Frederick. *Just Promoted!* New York: McGraw-Hill, 1992.

Booher, Dianna. *67 Presentations Secrets to Wow Any Audience.* Minneapolis, MN: Lakewood Publications, 1995.

———. *Clean Up Your Act!* New York: Warner Books, 1992.

———. *Communicate with Confidence! How to Say It Right the First Time and Every Time.* New York: McGraw-Hill, 1994.

———. *Cutting Paperwork in the Corporate Culture.* New York: Facts on File, 1986.

**219**

———. *First Thing Monday Morning*. Nashville: Thomas Nelson, 1992.

———. *Good Grief, Good Grammar: The Businessperson's Guide to Grammar and Usage*. New York: Facts on File, 1988.

———. *Send Me a Memo*. New York: Facts on File, 1984.

———. *Would You Put That in Writing?* New York: Facts on File, 1992.

Boyett, Joseph H., and Boyett, Jimmie T. *Beyond the Workplace 2000: Essential Strategies for the New American Corporation*. New York: Dutton, 1995.

Bridges, William. *JobShift: How to Prosper in a Workplace without Jobs*. Reading, MA: Addison-Wesley, 1994.

Briles, Judith, Ph.D. *Money Sense: What Every Woman Must Know to Be Financially Confident*. Chicago: Moody Press, 1995.

Calano, Jimmy, and Salzman, Jeff. *Careertracking: 26 Success Shortcuts to the Top*. New York: Simon & Schuster, 1988.

Cohen, William A., and Cohen, Nurit. *Top Executive Performance*. New York: John Wiley & Sons, 1984.

Collins, Eliza G. C., and Devanna, Mary Anne. *The Portable MBA*. New York: John Wiley & Sons, 1990.

Crosby, Philip B. *Leading: The Art of Becoming an Executive*. New York: McGraw-Hill, 1990.

Dawson, Roger. *The Confident Decision Maker*. New York: Morrow, 1993.

De Pree, Max. *Leadership Is an Art*. New York: Dell, 1989.

Downs, Alan. *The Ugly Truth about Layoffs—How Corporate Greed Is Shattering Lives, Companies, and Communities*. New York: Amacom Book Division, 1995.

Drucker, Peter F. *The Effective Executive*. New York: Harper & Row, 1966.

———. *Management: Tasks, Responsibilities, Practices*. New York: HarperCollins, 1993.

Dyer, William G. *Team Building: Issues and Alternatives*. Reading, MA: Addison-Wesley Publishing, 1977.

Epstein, Seymour, Ph.D., and Brodsky, Archie. *You're Smarter Than You Think: How to Develop Your Practical Intelligence for Success in Living*. New York: Simon & Schuster, 1993.

Ferrell, O.C., and Gareth Gardiner. *In Pursuit of Ethics: Tough Choices in the World of Work.* Springfield, IL: Smith Collins Co., 1991.

Fournies, Ferdinand F. *Coaching for Improved Work Performance.* New York: Van Nostrand Reinhold, 1987.

Garfield, Charles. "Ethics and Corporate Social Responsibility." *Executive Excellence*: August, 1995.

Glacel, Barbara Pate, and Robert, Emile A. Jr. *Light Bulbs for Leaders: A Guidebook for Team Learning.* New York: John Wiley & Sons, 1996.

Gladstein, Gerald. *Changing Careers: A 10-Year Demonstration of a Developmental Life-Span Approach.* Rochester, NY: University of Rochester Press, 1994.

Gow, Kathleen M., Ph.D. *Yes, Virginia, There Is Right and Wrong.* Wheaton, IL: Tyndale House, 1985.

Gray, James, Jr. *The Winning Image.* New York: Amacom Book Division, 1982.

Harmon, Frederick G. *The Executive Odyssey: Secrets for a Career without Limits.* New York: John Wiley & Sons, 1989.

Hind, James F. *The Heart & Soul of Effective Management.* Wheaton, IL: Victor, 1973.

Hyatt, Carole. *Lifetime Employability.* New York: Mastermedia, 1995.

Kanter, Rosabeth Moss, Ph.D. *Men and Women of the Corporation.* New York: Basic Books, Inc., 1977.

Kao, John J. *The Entrepreneur.* Englewood Cliffs, NJ: Prentice Hall, 1991.

Kotter, John P. *The Leadership Factor.* New York: The Free Press, 1988.

Levine, Stuart R. *The Leader in You: How to Win Friends, Influence People, and Succeed in a Changing World.* New York: Simon & Schuster, 1993.

Livingstone, John Leslie. *The Portable MBA in Finance and Accounting.* New York: John Wiley & Sons, 1992.

Lombardo, Michael, McCall, Morgan W. Jr., and Morrison, Ann M. *The Lessons of Experience: How Successful Execs Develop on the Job.* Lexington, MA: Lexington Press, 1989.

McCormack, Mark H. *What They Don't Teach You at Harvard Business School*. New York: Bantam, 1984.

Morrisey, George. *Morrisey on Planning: A Guide to Strategic Thinking*. San Francisco: Jossey-Bass, 1996.

Noe, John R. *Peak Performance Principles for High Achievers*. New York: Berkeley Books, 1984.

Olesen, Erik. *Twelve Steps to Mastering the Winds of Change: Peak Performers Reveal How to Stay on Top*. New York: MacMillan, 1993.

Parker, Glenn M. *Team Players and Teamwork*. San Francisco: Jossey-Bass, 1990.

Parson, Mary Jean. *An Executive's Coaching Handbook*. Ann Arbor, MI: Books on Demand.

Peck, M. Scott, M.D. *The Road Less Traveled*. New York: Simon & Schuster, 1978.

Pennington, Randy S. "From Ethics to Integrity." *Executive Excellence*: August, 1995.

Pfau, Bruce, Ph.D. *1995-6 Hay Employee Attitudes Study*. Wellesley, MA: Hay Research for Management, June, 1995.

Pritchett, Price. *The Employee Handbook of New Work Habits for a Radically Changing World: 13 Ground Rules for Job Success in the Information Age*. Dallas: Pritchett Publishing Company, 1994.

Rasberry, Salli, and Selwyn, Padi. *Living Your Life Out Loud*. New York: Pocket Books, 1995.

Scheele, Adele M., Ph.D. *Skills for Success: A Guide to the Top for Men and Women*. New York: Ballantine Books, 1988.

Scott, Dru. *How to Put More Time in Your Life*. New York: Rawson, Wade, 1980.

Senge, Peter M. *The Fifth Discipline: The Art and Practice of the Learning Organization*. New York: Doubleday, 1990.

Shimer, Porter. *Fitness through Pleasure*. Emmaus, PA: Rodale Press, 1982.

Silk, Leonard Solomon. *Ethics and Profits: The Crisis of Confidence in American Business*. New York: Simon & Schuster, 1976.

Sloma, Richard S. *No-Nonsense Planning.* New York: The Free Press, 1984.

Stern, Barbara B., Ph. D. *Is Networking for You? A Working Woman's Alternative to the Old Boy System.* Englewood Cliffs, NJ: Prentice-Hall, 1981.

Stewart, Nathaniel. *The Effective Woman Manager: 7 Vital Skills for Upward Mobility.* New York: Ballantine, 1978.

Stowell, Steven J., and Starcevich, Matt M., Ph.D. *The Coach: Creating Partnerships for a Competitive Edge.* Salt Lake City, UT: Center for Management and Organizational Effectiveness, 1987.

Townsend, Robert. *Up the Organization.* New York: Knopf, 1970.

Tracy, Brian. *Maximum Achievement.* New York: Simon & Schuster, 1993.

Tracy, Diane. *Take This Job and Love It: A Personal Guide to Career Empowerment.* New York: McGraw-Hill, 1994.

Tuleja, Tad, and Tarkenton, Fran. *How to Motivate People.* New York: Harper & Row, 1986.

Unell, Barbara C., and Wyckoff, Jerry L. *20 Teachable Virtues.* New York: Berkley/Perigee, 1995.

Uris, Auren. *101 of the Greatest Ideas in Management.* New York: John Wiley & Sons, 1986.

———. *The Executive Deskbook.* New York: Van Nostrand Reinhold, 1970.

U.S. Department Secretary's Commission on Achieving Necessary Skills. *Learning a Living: A Blueprint for High Performance: A SCANS Report for America 2000.* Washington, D.C.: Discovery Publications, April, 1992.

Wellins, Richard S., Schaaf, Dick, and Shomo, Kathy. *Succeeding with Teams: 101 Tips That Really Work.* Minneapolis, MN: Lakewood Publications, 1994.

Winston, Stephanie. *The Organized Executive: Program for Productivity: New Ways to Manage Time, Paper, and People.* New York: Warner, 1990.

# Other Resources by Dianna Booher

## BOOKS

Communicate with Confidence: How to Say It Right the First Time & Every Time

The Complete Letterwriter's Almanac

Executive's Portfolio of Model Speeches for All Occasions

Fresh-Cut Flowers for a Friend

Get a Life without Sacrificing Your Career

Great Personal Letters for Busy People

Good Grief, Good Grammar

The New Secretary: How to Handle People as Well as You Handle Paper

To the Letter: A Handbook of Model Letters for the Busy Executive

Send Me a Memo

Winning Sales Letters

Clean Up Your Act

Writing for Technical Professionals

Would You Put That in Writing?

67 Presentation Secrets to Wow Any Audience

## VIDEOTAPES

Basic Steps for Better Business Writing (series)

Business Writing: Quick, Clear, Concise

Closing the Gap: Gender Communication Skills

Cutting Paperwork: Management Strategies

Cutting Paperwork: Support Staff Strategies

## AUDIOTAPE SERIES

Get Your Book Published

People Power

Write to the Point: Business Communications from Memos to Meetings

## SOFTWARE (DISKS AND CD-ROM)

Effective Editing

Effective Writing

Good Grief, Good Grammar

More Good Grief, Good Grammar

Model Business Letters

Model Personal Letters

Model Sales Letters

Model Speeches and Toasts

Ready, Set, NeGOtiate

## WORKSHOPS

Customer Service Communications

Developing Winning Proposals

Effective Writing

Technical Writing

Good Grief, Good Grammar

Leading and Participating in Productive Meetings

Listening Until You Really Hear

Negotiating So That Everyone Feels Like a Winner

People Power (interpersonal skills)

People Productivity (interpersonal skills)

Presentations That Work

Resolving Conflict without Punching Someone Out

## SPEECHES

Communicating CARE to Customers

Communication: From Boardroom to Bedroom

Communication: The 10 Cs

The Gender Communication Gap: "Did You Hear What I Think I Said?"

Get a Life without Sacrificing Your Career

The Plan and the Purpose—Despite the Pain and the Pace

Platform Tips for the Presenter

Putting Together the Puzzle of Personal Excellence

Write This Way to Success

You Are Your Future: Employable for a Lifetime

## FOR MORE INFORMATION

Booher Consultants, Inc.
4001 Gateway Dr.
Colleyville, TX 76034-5917
Phone: 817-318-6000
Booher@compuserve.com

Dianna Booher and her staff travel internationally, speaking and presenting seminars and training workshops on communication and motivational topics.

# Index

Systems and procedures, activity for, 69-71

# About the Author

Dianna Booher is an internationally recognized business communication expert and the author of 32 books and numerous audios, videos, CD-ROMs, and an entire suite of software to increase communication effectiveness and productivity. She is the founder and president of Booher Consultants, based in the Dallas-Fort Worth metroplex. Her firm provides communication training to some of the largest Fortune 500 companies and government agencies: IBM, Exxon, Mobil, Hewlett-Packard, Pennzoil, AMR, Frito-Lay, Apple Computer, Blue Cross and Blue Shield, Coopers & Lybrand, Deloitte & Touche, Texas Instruments, NASA, and MCI, to name just a few.